The high cost of following Christ is a major theme in the Gospels. A fickle or indifferent disciple is a contradiction. And Christ's own summons to discipleship is impossible to harmonize with the laid-back, seeker-sensitive, superficial religion practiced by so many people today who claim to be followers of Christ. Believers constantly need to be reminded of these truths. Dr. Lawson's exposition of Luke 14:25-35 distills the vital message and presents it in a robust and penetrating way. Here is a book every Christian ought to read and seriously take to heart.

JOHN MACARTHUR
President, The Master's University and Seminary
Pastor-Teacher, Grace Community Church, Sun Valley, California

With compassion, patience, and clarity, Dr. Lawson sets before the reader a clear exposition of the gospel and the gospel call according to Jesus. He writes as he preaches—with a tenacious grip on the Scriptures and a pastor's heart that longs for the salvation of the lost and the edification of the church. This book is a 'must read' for all! The unconverted will hear the gospel; the Christian will find the true road to devotion and joy; the minister will be instructed in the task of biblical gospel preaching, ensuring salvation both for himself and for those who hear him (1 Tim. 4:16).

PAUL WASHER
President, Heart Cry Ministry, Radford, Virginia

Like a master builder Steve Lawson gives us the foundation of Jesus' own words to erect a frame showing the cost, demands, gains and losses of following Christ. In doing so, Dr. Lawson gives us a strong and firm edifice that brings glory to Him and His truth.

R. C. SPROUL (1939–2017)
Founder and Former Chairman of Ligonier Ministries,
Former Chancellor of Reformation Bible College, Sanford, Florida

There are books that you read, and then there are books that read you. This is one of the latter—a book that searches your heart because it exposes you to the holy and compassionate gaze of Jesus Christ. In this little gem, Dr. Lawson helps you honestly count the cost of what it means to be a disciple of our Lord. In these pages, Jesus comes to you and me asking, 'Are you truly my disciple? Am I your all in all?' Blessed are those who, after reading this book, can truly confess that the Holy Spirit witnesses with their spirit on a biblical foundation that they are the children of God.

JOEL R. BEEKE
President, Puritan Reformed Theological Seminary, Grand Rapids, Michigan

IT WILL

COST

YOU

EVERY

THING

WHAT IT TAKES TO FOLLOW JESUS

STEVEN J. LAWSON

CHRISTIAN
FOCUS

Copyright © 2021 Steven J. Lawson

hardback ISBN 978-1-5271-0703-8
mobi ISBN 978-1-5271-0716-8
epub ISBN 978-1-5271-0717-5

10 9 8 7 6 5 4 3 2

First published in 2017 under the title
The Cost (paperback ISBN 978-1-7819-1955-2)
This new edition published in 2021

Reprinted in 2021, 2022 (twice) and 2024
by
Christian Focus Publications Ltd,
Geanies House, Fearn, Tain, Ross-shire,
Scotland IV20 1TW, UK.

www.christianfocus.com

Cover design by Pete Barnsley

Cover photo by: František G. on Unsplash

Printed by Gutenberg

CONTENTS

DEDICATED TO

AUSTIN T. DUNCAN,
A FAITHFUL FRIEND IN MINISTRY,
AN INVALUABLE ASSET,
AND CONSTANT ENCOURAGER

Preface

During my senior year in high school, I was offered a four-year football scholarship to play for Texas Tech University, well known for its strong athletic program.

As soon as I signed the agreement, everything for my college education was entirely covered for the rest of my time there. My tuition was free. My room was free. My meals were free. My laundry was free. My books were free. My travel home was free. My tutors were free. For the next four years, my entire college education was paid in full. It did not cost me a single dime.

But the moment I signed the contract, it cost me everything.

I was committed to twice a day practices under the blazing hot sun in West Texas. There were full contact scrimmages. Wind sprints. Agility drills. Weightlifting. Running laps. Tackling drills. Blocking drills. Climbing stadium steps.

Off the field, I was devoted to team meetings. Team rules. Curfew hours. Class attendance. Required grades. Even church attendance.

In many senses, the coaches of the football team owned me. They told me when I would wake up. When I would go to sleep. When I would eat. When I would arrive at practice. When I was expected at team meetings. When I could fly home for holidays. And when I would return to campus. I had no life of my own. They owned me.

This free education cost me everything. It required trips to the hospital. Sessions with the athletic trainer. To say nothing of my blood and sweat. Toil and tears. It cost me sleep. I gave up free time. In return, I received injuries. I hobbled to class on crutches. I endured much pain.

None of this sacrifice was optional. All of it was mandatory. Again, my college education was entirely free. But it cost me everything.

In a real way, this is a picture of our salvation in Jesus Christ. All our sins were paid in full by the sinless life and substitutionary death of Jesus Christ upon the cross. We contribute nothing. His finished work is complete. Nothing is left for us to contribute. Forgiveness is offered as a free, pre-paid gift.

Yet at the same time, the cost of following Christ comes at a high price.

It will require a life of self-denial. Death to self. Submission to Christ. Sacrifice for His kingdom. Adversity in life. Tribulation for your faith. Rejection from friends. Persecution from the world. And maybe even martyrdom.

Salvation is entirely free. But receiving it will cost you everything. It is not offered as cheap grace. Nor is it received by easy believism. It does not take a particularly special person to be a Christian. Just all there is of him.

This book is a walk through a challenging passage of Scripture, Luke 14:25-35. This biblical account contains some of the hard sayings of Christ. They are hard to hear. Hard to take. Hard to receive.

But these words of Christ yield vast eternal dividends. They promise unimaginable spiritual riches. They lead to treasure houses of divine blessings. The sacrifice of all you have yields infinite rewards. The cost is truly worth it.

In this important passage, Jesus specifically lays out what it means to follow Him. I trust that in this book, you will come to a clearer understanding of the high cost of discipleship for your life.

May you answer the Master's call to follow Him—on His terms.

Blessings in Christ,

Steven J. Lawson
Dallas, TX

1

COME FOLLOW

'Come after Me' (Luke 14:27).

To follow Jesus Christ is the greatest adventure you could ever undertake. Pursuing Him fulfills your greatest purpose, which is to magnify His glory. Trusting Him meets your greatest need, namely, the forgiveness of sin. Loving Christ gives you the greatest pleasure, the supreme joy of knowing Him.

Being taught by Christ gives you the greatest wisdom, the divine truth that He alone possesses. Abiding in Him imparts the greatest power, His all-sufficient grace for daily living. Walking with Him provides you with the greatest fellowship, the sheer delight of communing with Him. And traveling this one path leads to the greatest destination beyond this life—into His immediate presence in heaven.

There is no journey that can compare with this one. Pursuing Christ will take you from where you are to where you need to be. It will take you through all of life's many experiences, from your greatest moments to your darkest nights, with Jesus by your side. As you follow in His footsteps, you will discover the abundant life He came to give. And it will ultimately lead you home to heaven, to the very throne of God. No pursuit in life can compare to this journey of following Jesus.

A Spiritual Journey

When Jesus calls you to come after Him, He is comparing the Christian life to the path that you must walk. He personally invites you to embark on this spiritual journey. By this summons, He is not calling you to a mere *physical* walk with Him. He is not urging you to put one foot in front of the other and, literally, keep in step with Him. What He is requiring is far deeper than for you to travel a dusty road with Him. He is instead speaking in spiritual terms. He is inviting you to follow Him in your heart. He is calling you to take steps of faith and follow His direction for your life.

This spiritual journey determines how you live your daily life. It concerns the direction that you take in life. Jesus is referring to the road you take in this world. Involved in this journey are your motives, desires, thoughts, choices, and actions. Jesus is addressing what is driving and directing you.

When the Master Calls

Our focus will be upon one particular encounter that Jesus had with a large crowd that was accompanying Him. For the most part, they gave every impression of being His disciples. They were walking with Him and were attentive to His words. They had close proximity to Him. But the reality was that most of them were only curious about Jesus and largely remained uncommitted—and unconverted.

Following Jesus had become the popular thing to do, and He knew it. With a genuine concern for them, Christ stopped and turned around to address them. His words were strong as He made it not easier, but harder, to follow Him. Jesus called for the full-scale commitment of their lives to Him when He said:

'If anyone comes to Me, and does not hate his own father and mother and wife and children and brothers and sisters, yes, and even his own life, he cannot be My disciple. Whoever does not carry his own cross and come after Me cannot be My disciple. For which one of you, when he wants to build a tower, does not first sit down and calculate the cost to see if he has enough to complete it? Otherwise, when he has laid a foundation and is not able to finish, all who observe it begin to ridicule him, saying, 'This man began to build and was not able to finish.' Or what king, when he sets out to meet another king in battle, will not first sit down and consider whether he is strong enough with ten thousand *men* to encounter the one coming against him with twenty thousand? Or else, while the other is still far away, he sends a delegation and asks for terms of peace. So then, none of you can be

My disciple who does not give up all his own possessions. 'Therefore, salt is good; but if even salt has become tasteless, with what will it be seasoned? It is useless either for the soil or for the manure pile; it is thrown out. He who has ears to hear, let him hear' (Luke 14:26-35).

Not Sugar-coated

These provocative words were spoken near the end of Jesus' three-year ministry, during His final journey to Jerusalem. In only a few months, He would be crucified upon a Roman cross in this very city, which was the headquarters for the religious establishment in Israel. Jesus knew He had little time remaining on this earth. This was not a moment to mince words. Nor a time to sugar-coat the message. Jesus was not here to smooth-talk the crowd. The issues were too great, and the time was too short.

In this critical moment, Jesus spoke words that were direct and demanding. They were no doubt difficult for His followers to hear. But these words were necessary and appropriate to the moment. His forceful tone was demanded by the eternal weight of the subject matter. The impact of these words was intended to awaken the spiritually dead among them. Jesus had to speak as He did in order to capture those who were lethargic. He called them to follow Him in a new journey that would one day lead them to the throne of God. What Jesus said to His listeners, He now says to you.

Where the Journey Begins

This journey of faith begins the moment you come to faith in Jesus Christ. Becoming a follower of Jesus starts when you first devote your life to Him. This new relationship does not commence when you simply join a religious crowd. Nor when you try to become a good person. Instead, it starts when you come to entrust your life to Him.

To begin this journey costs you nothing. There is no amount of good works you could ever perform that could earn you a place on this narrow path. There is no toll fee for you to pay to enter onto it. There is no moral standard for you to meet. There is no spiritual ladder for you to climb. There are no rituals for you to perform. There are no ceremonies for you to attend. There is absolutely nothing you can do to merit starting this journey with Christ.

You may only enter into this spiritual relationship by faith. The Bible says: 'For by grace you have been saved through faith; and that not of yourselves, *it is* the gift of God; not as a result of works, so that no one may boast' (Eph. 2:8-9). This could not be any clearer. Entering this journey cannot be earned by your good works. Instead, it is entered into by faith in Him.

How the Journey Continues

This commitment to Jesus Christ is the beginning of a whole new life. Previously, you had been walking according to the course of this world. You had been going in the direction of the world. You were in a life pursuit of doing your own thing. You did what you wanted, how you wanted, when you wanted, with whom you wanted. You were traveling on the broad path that accommodated any manner of life. But when you come to Christ by faith, this new journey begins that takes you in an entirely new direction.

Following Jesus means we no longer go our own way. We no longer follow the flow of the crowd. We begin to walk a new path that is headed in a new direction. We walk as Jesus walked and imitate Him. We start to obey the Word of God as Jesus did while He was here on the earth. We are to love people as He loved, even those who are most difficult to love. We are to act as He acted and react as He reacted in each situation. We are to meet the many challenges in life as He did, with supreme confidence in God.

What the Journey Provides

Following Jesus on this journey leads you into the greatest life you could ever live. When you commit your life to Him, you receive the immediate forgiveness of your sins. The penalties for your transgressions are completely removed. All charges brought against you are cancelled. You are clothed with the perfect righteousness of Christ. You are given full acceptance with holy God in heaven. You are set free from your bondage to sin. Christ comes to live in you, never to leave you.

Coming after Christ will directly lead you into the will of God. The path that God has chosen leads to the abundant life that only Jesus can give. Following Jesus leads you into the fullness of God's blessings. When you walk with Him, He promises deep contentment and true happiness (Matt. 5:3-12). Jesus gives the Holy Spirit, who gives the strength to walk with Him (John 14:16-17). The Spirit is 'another Helper' who will advise and guide you on the chosen path. The Spirit will comfort you when you are discouraged. He will exhort you when you are complacent. And He will convict you when you stray.

Jesus further gives you His peace, unlike anything this world can give (John 14:27). This peace is His calming tranquility in the midst of your many difficulties. Jesus gives true joy (John 15:11). He enables you to live triumphantly in the face of many challenges. He gives you His fellowship as you walk with Him daily. He provides you with His direction through the confusing maze of this world. He provides for all your needs according to His riches in glory, and causes everything to work together for your good.

What the Journey Costs

However, following Jesus is a lifelong journey that comes at a high price. This is not a relationship to be entered into lightly. This decision requires the commitment of your entire life to Him. Coming to Christ demands highest priority over every other aspect of your life. It necessitates the submission of your will to His lordship. This path requires your sacrifice and even your willingness to suffer for Him.

To be sure, Jesus will not follow you—you are called to follow Him.

Following Christ will cost you much. It will cost you your old way of life and forfeiting your past sins. It will cost you a life of ease and living for this world. It will cost you old habits and old associations. It will cost you following your own agenda for your life. It will cost you time and treasure. It will cost you suffering for being identified with Him. It will cost you opposition and persecution from the world. It may even cost you your life. But in the end, you gain far more than you lose.

Where the Journey Leads

This journey, nevertheless, leads to the glories of heaven, where Christ Himself is seated at the right hand of God the Father. Following Jesus will usher us into His immediate presence in the world to come. It leads us to a new home in heaven where He is being worshiped by all believers who have put their faith in Him. This journey will lead us to where an untold number of angels are praising Him.

No other journey leads to such a glorious destination. This path leads us upward to a far better place than this world. It ushers us to the heights of heaven. It brings us to the presence of God.

Where Are You?

Let me ask you: Where are *you* in this spiritual journey with Jesus Christ? Have you begun this journey yet? Are you a genuine follower of Jesus? Are you on this walk with Him? Have you entrusted your life to Him? Or are you merely curious?

If you are not a follower of Jesus, the message that He delivered is given especially for you. Contained in this address is how to start this journey of faith. Here is how to take the first step in walking with Him. These words by Jesus reveal the entry point into a personal relationship with Him.

What Jesus said so long ago is the most important message you will ever hear. This truth requires something from you. These words spoken by Jesus are not intended to be merely interesting. They are meant to capture your life and secure your soul. They are intended to enlist you to become a true follower of Christ.

What Jesus says in these words will challenge the faith of every authentic disciple. This message should deepen your resolve to follow Christ. If you are a believer, you should reaffirm your foundational commitment to Him. Here are necessary elements for your true spirituality and growth in Christlikeness.

This Is for You

No matter where you are in life, these words from Jesus are intended for you. His words are just as relevant today as when He first spoke them. It is worth your undivided attention to embrace every statement Jesus made to this crowd. Here are life-giving words from the One who is the way, the truth, and the life—Jesus Christ our Lord.

Mixed Multitudes

Now large crowds were going along
with Him (Luke 14:25).

Large crowds can be an easy place to hide. The larger the
crowd, the easier it is to remain anonymous. The more
people gather together, the easier it is to blend in with the
masses. The bigger the assemblage, the easier it is to remain
undetected. This was certainly the case with the large
crowds that were following Jesus Christ.

As Jesus was journeying toward Jerusalem, He was
headed to the very city where He would be eventually
crucified. On this final trip to the holy city, massive crowds

were following Him. The biblical text reads that 'large crowds' were going along with Him. This group was more than a handful of people. This was an enormous convergence of humanity. This states that 'large crowds' in the plural were walking with Him. The sum total of all these large crowds, collectively, comprised a vast sea of men, women, and children.

The Final Journey

For Jesus, death upon a Roman cross lay directly ahead of Him. The excruciating pain of Calvary was only months away. This would be His final journey to the holy city. Here was His last trip to the nerve center of the religious establishment. As Jesus would address this crowd, this was no time to pull up short with His message. This is a passing opportunity to address these people.

This tremendous throng was a diverse group. They were all merged together to form one enormous multitude. The swelling numbers formed a huge mass of humanity that was walking behind Him. The excitement level of the crowd was escalating as Jesus was the most compelling figure of the day. Everyone wanted to see Him with their own eyes. Everyone wanted to hear His teaching in person.

A Diverse Crowd

In this diverse group were all kinds of people, who were at different places in life. Some of Jesus' followers were genuinely committed to Him. They had left behind their old ways of life and had surrendered to Him. They had entered into a new life, as they were following Him with wholehearted devotion. These were true followers who believed He was the Son of God come to rescue ruined humanity.

Other people in the crowd were merely curious. They had never seen or heard anyone like Jesus. They were drawn to Him because He was so unlike the other religious leaders. He did not quote the other rabbis, but spoke with direct authority from God Himself. They referred to Him as Rabbi and recognized Him as a teacher come from God. They hung upon His every word, though they were still not convinced by them.

Still others were confused about who He was. Is this not the carpenter's son? Is not His mother called Mary? Could any good thing come from His hometown of Nazareth? Does He have an unclean spirit? This could not be the long-awaited Messiah, could it? Was He something more? In their confusion, they remained uncommitted.

Yet others in this large multitude were intensely religious, entrapped in the false system of the Pharisees. They had the outward form of religion, but not the inward reality of knowing God. They were unconverted—religious, but lost. What is worse, they did not know that they were without God.

I want us to look at these groups more carefully. As we do, you may see yourself in one of these categories.

The Committed Few

The first group in this large crowd were the *committed* disciples. They are the ones who were genuinely converted. At least eleven of the twelve disciples were true believers in Him. The Lord had called them to leave behind their old lives and follow Him on this new path. He had summoned them to leave behind their past pursuits of living for themselves. Now they must live for Him. Eleven of these men had answered that compelling call. They took the radical step of faith to follow Him.

Jesus first had invited two fishermen—John and Andrew—to stay with Him (John 1:35-39). They responded by giving their lives to Him. Andrew then brought his brother Simon to Jesus, who was also converted (John 1:40-42). Jesus then called Philip, saying 'Follow Me' (John 1:43). Philip answered the call, and then found Nathaniel (John 1:45), who became a genuine disciple.

Jesus called a tax collector named Matthew to follow Him (Matt. 9:9). This despised publican had been living in a world of greed. He existed to accumulate the possessions of this world. But in that moment, he made the life-altering decision to turn his back on his old priorities. He instantly surrendered his life to Christ. There would be no turning back.

The Radical Choice

The rest of the disciples—Thomas, Bartholomew, Thaddeus, James the lesser, and Simon (Mark 3:18)—made the radical choice to submit their lives to the lordship of Jesus Christ. They left behind all for which they had previously lived. Like a traveler approaching a major fork in the road, they abandoned the broad path and entered through the narrow gate. They forsook the many to join the few. In that defining moment, they stepped out with decisive faith to follow Him.

Have you forsaken your old way of life? Have you received the new life that Jesus offers? Have you decided to follow Christ? If so, you are on the right path with the right crowd, headed in the right direction.

The Curious Majority

The second group in this crowd were merely curious about this popular religious figure named Jesus. They were undoubtedly attracted to Him by the remarkable things they had heard others say about Him. They had heard the reports about His miracles. Some had seen Him perform them. Others had heard the reports that God was with Him. He spoke as no man had ever spoken before. They had heard that He claimed to be the Son of God. Their curiosity was piqued and they had to check it out for themselves.

Many such people were drawn to follow Jesus. Perhaps most of the crowd. They wanted to see if these claims were true. Were the reports valid that they had heard? Could this be the long-awaited Messiah? Is Jesus really the Son of God as He claims to be? These inquisitive spectators had to see it for themselves. This would have comprised a large segment of those around Jesus.

The Same Today

Countless people today are like this. They are drawn to Christ out of curiosity. They are interested in Jesus because He remains the central figure of human history. Many are intrigued with what He says about the issues of the day. They see the good that is being done in His name. They are impressed with the Christian hospitals. They see Christian ministries serving the needs of humanity. They enjoy the festivities of Christian holidays like Christmas and Easter.

However, these inquisitive individuals have not committed their lives to Jesus. They are merely interested in the mystique surrounding Him. They are drawn to the uniqueness of Christ. They are simply a part of the crowd going along with Him. But they have never surrendered their lives to Him.

I wonder if this could describe you? Are you interested to learn more about Jesus Christ? You realize there has to be something more to life than what you have experienced. Perhaps you sense the emptiness of this world and feel the void of being merely religious. Maybe you are giving thought to standing before God after death. Maybe you want to know what will happen when you face Him.

If this describes you, then you should give careful consideration to what Jesus has to say. He alone is the source of truth that will lead you into the eternal life that only He can give.

The Confused Masses

There was also a third group in the crowd following Jesus. They were perplexed about who He was. They simply could not swallow His claims to be divine. Was He not a man like them? Neither could they figure out why He came into the world. They presumed He was merely a prophet from God. They thought He was a wise sage with profound insights into the complexities of life. They saw Him as a good man, whose life should be emulated, but nothing beyond this.

This segment of the large crowd was also confused about the way of salvation. They presumed that the interpretation of the Pharisees was right. Surely, good people work their way to heaven. These religious leaders had convinced them that they must keep the divine Law in order to gain favor with God. But they had misjudged the absolute perfection needed to enter heaven. They could not grasp that they could not keep it, yet they continued to try.

Faulty Perceptions

Many people are exactly like this today. They presume that they must accomplish a prescribed amount of good works to gain acceptance with God. How much? They do not know. Tragically, nothing could be further from the truth. They do not understand that all have fallen short of the glory of God (Rom. 3:23). Instead, they wrongly cling to the hope that God grades on a curve. If they are better than others, they presume they will pass the grade.

Does this faulty perception about salvation describe you? Maybe you are unclear about what is required. Perhaps you are uncertain about how to obtain forgiveness of sin. Maybe you are confused about what the hard sayings of Jesus mean about entrance into His kingdom. The different religious voices you are hearing may leave you uncertain about whom to believe. If this describes you, you must listen to what Jesus said in this encounter with the crowd.

The Convicted Seekers

A fourth group would have been a part of this massive throng of people. These were people actually seeking to learn more about Jesus Christ and salvation. They had heard Him preach about the kingdom of God and were processing what He had taught. Among this part of this multitude were individuals who were coming under the conviction of their sin. They were becoming acutely aware of their need for the forgiveness Jesus was offering.

These convicted seekers knew that they had an empty soul. A deep restlessness was provoking them to follow this new Teacher. They undoubtedly felt guilty because they knew they fell short of the divine standard in the Law. They were persuaded that they did not measure up to what God required. But what were they to do?

Painfully Aware

A loud alarm was sounding within their troubled consciences. They were painfully aware that something was not right between them and God. Something was missing. As they heard Jesus speak, they heard that they needed to commit their lives to Him. They learned they needed to respond to His free offer to enter the kingdom of God. But they had not yet responded to this invitation. They were not yet ready to make this choice. The enormity of this decision was dawning upon them. But they felt they could not walk away from their old ways. They stood at the crossroads of life.

This is precisely where many people stand today. Perhaps even you. You know that whatever you have experienced to this point has not been the real thing. You recognize the haunting conviction of your sin that will not go away. You know you need the forgiveness of sin. Maybe you continue to follow with the religious crowd that gathers at church. Maybe you are a part of a small group Bible study. Or maybe you continue to talk about spiritual things with another person at work. But you are not yet there. You have not made the decision to become an authentic follower of Christ.

Could this describe where you are right now?

The Counterfeit Followers

In these large crowds, there was a fifth category of people. These gave the appearance of being genuine disciples. They were adept at blending in with the religious crowd. They knew the right words to use to sound spiritual. They were deft at masking their own spiritual void. They enjoyed this close proximity to Jesus. They even traveled with Him. They were not lagging behind at a distance. They were actually right next to Jesus.

In reality, though, they were not authentic believers in Jesus Christ. They were merely caught up in the excitement of this movement. Truth be known, they had a superficial attachment to Jesus. They had an empty testimony in Christ. They knew about Christ, but they did not know Him.

One Like Judas

One such follower was a man named Judas. He was a charter member of the inner circle around Jesus. He was one of the twelve disciples who ate and lived with Jesus. Judas was as involved in ministry as anyone else could be. He was privy to the inner workings of the kingdom. He observed firsthand the personal integrity in Christ. He heard the profound truths that Jesus taught. He witnessed the powerful miracles that Jesus performed. He saw the people whose lives had been dramatically transformed. He was so highly respected by the other eleven disciples that they made him the treasurer in charge of their money.

Yet despite all this advantage, Judas remained a counterfeit disciple. He had perfected the art of acting religious. He had a safe hiding place in the shadows of Jesus. But in his heart, he remained uncommitted to Christ. Judas had never died to self. He continued to pursue his own selfish interests. The chief pursuit of his life remained himself. He wanted Jesus on his own terms. He saw Jesus as a means for personal gain. He had no desire to be sold out to Jesus—only to sell Him. In fact, when the opportunity arose, Judas sold Jesus to the religious leaders of Israel. Tragically, Judas remained outside the kingdom of God. He had become so skilled at looking religious that no one knew his hypocrisy. He even fooled himself.

Perhaps You?

Could this describe your life? Perhaps people think of you as a Christian. But could it be that you are not? Maybe you grew up in a Christian home. Maybe you have been baptized and joined the church. Maybe you regularly attend a Bible study. But could it be that you have never surrendered your life to Jesus Christ? Jesus demands that entrance into His kingdom requires that you submit your life to Him.

Could you be self-deceived about where you stand with God? There are large numbers of people who live under this false delusion regarding their spiritual state. Could you be one of these counterfeit converts?

Where Do You See Yourself?

These are the same categories of people today who are going along with Jesus Christ. Nothing has changed over the centuries. This same diverse crowd is following Him with varying interest in what He says. Few are committed. Some are merely curious. Many are confused. Others are self-deceived.

Each one of us needs to ask ourselves, 'Where do I see myself in a gathering like this?' You need to examine yourself and determine where you are in your relationship to Jesus Christ. Where the different people were two thousand years ago is where many find themselves today. Nothing has changed over the centuries.

A Right Diagnosis

In the medical world, it is said that a right diagnosis is half the cure. The same is true in the spiritual realm. It is absolutely imperative that you have an accurate diagnosis of where you stand with the Lord. A right assessment of where your life stands in relationship to Jesus Christ is critical. You must know where you are before you can know what you need—and what you need to do.

In the following chapters, we will carefully analyze what is required to be a genuine follower of Jesus Christ. In the next chapter, we will discover what Jesus said. But I must warn you. What you will read are strong words from the lips of the Lord. I hope you are sitting down.

SHOCKING WORDS

If anyone comes to Me, and does not
hate his own father and mother and
wife and children and brothers and
sisters, yes, and even his own life, he
cannot be My disciple
(Luke 14:26).

Jesus Christ was a straight-talker. He always told it like it is.
He never minced words or beat around the bush. Whatever
controversy surrounded His ministry, it was rarely because He
was misunderstood. The very opposite was usually the case.
Trouble followed Him because He was explicit in what He said.
His words were not hard to understand—just hard to swallow.

What Jesus said to this particular crowd would easily
rank among the most shocking words ever to come from
His lips. This jolting statement was one of the hardest

hitting sayings He ever uttered. This abrasive assertion was one of the most demanding sayings He ever issued. These provocative words require a teachable spirit to receive them. When Jesus stopped to address this multitude, here is how He began: 'If anyone comes to Me, and does not hate his own father and mother and wife and children and brothers and sisters, yes, and even his own life, he cannot be My disciple' (v. 26). These are sobering words that the Lord spoke that day.

Jesus maintained that those who would be His followers must *hate* those whom they love the most. Did we hear that right? The Lord claimed that following Him requires hating the very ones who brought them into the world. Can this be right? They must hate their own spouse to whom they have unconditionally pledged to support. They must hate their own children who bear their own resemblance. Did Jesus really say that? Then Jesus goes one step further and makes an even greater demand. This plunges His sharp words yet deeper into their souls. Jesus added that anyone who would be His disciple must hate his or her own life. Say that again?

What Does This Mean?

What did Jesus mean by these seemingly harsh words? Does this not contradict so much else of what He taught? Does not the fifth commandment say that we are to honor our father and mother (Exod. 20:11)? Yes, the Law teaches this. Did not Moses write that we are to love our neighbor as we love ourselves (Lev. 19:18)? Certainly, he did. Did not Jesus command us to love our enemies (Matt. 22:39-40)? Yes, He did. Did not Jesus Himself care for His own mother as He hung upon the cross (John 19:27)? Of course He did. Did not Paul issue the imperative that husbands are to love their wives as Christ loved the church (Eph. 5:25)? Absolutely. Does not the Bible maintain that if a man does not provide for the members of his own household, he is worse than an infidel (1 Tim. 5:8)? Yes and amen.

A Right Interpretation

The challenge for us is to rightly interpret these provocative words from Christ. How do we harmonize this statement with the Scripture we just cited? How do we square these words with everything else that the Bible teaches? At first glance, this demand by Jesus seems to contradict the rest of the Bible. How are we to take this hard saying of Jesus?

This apparent contradiction can be resolved. The riddle can be easily solved. But first, let us consider how the hard saying begins.

An Open Invitation to All

Jesus begins this invitation by saying: 'If anyone comes to Me' (v. 26). When He says 'anyone,' He extended this offer to everyone in the crowd. This was an open appeal that He issued to all people under the sound of His voice. It was extended to everyone that day, regardless of their past. It went out to all, whether they were religious or irreligious. Moral or immoral. Cultured or uncouth. Here is the free offer of the gospel to everyone in the crowd. Jesus might as well have said, 'whosoever.' No one was excluded from this open-armed invitation.

This broad appeal issued by Christ to come and follow Him is still being extended down through the centuries. Even to us today. It is being offered to every person this moment. This includes *you*. You are being personally invited by Jesus Himself. To this day, Christ is still calling individuals, from far and wide, to become His disciples.

The Savior Calls

This call to come to Jesus necessitated that those in this crowd must take this decisive step of faith to come to Him. That is, they must commit their lives to Him. To come to Christ is the same as placing their whole life into His hands. It means to transfer their self-reliance for salvation to Him. This is the only way to have a right standing before God. In another passage, Jesus said, 'I am the bread of life; he who *comes* to Me will not hunger, and he who *believes* in Me will never thirst' (emphasis mine, John 6:35). Here, we see that coming to Jesus is the same as believing in Him.

Elsewhere, Jesus said, 'If anyone is thirsty, let him *come* to Me and drink' (emphasis mine, John 7:37b). Just as a person would thirst for water, draw it up to their mouth, and drink it, Jesus called the crowd to come to Him in order to receive eternal life. They must long for Him and receive Him into their souls. He alone can satisfy the deepest thirsting of their souls. One sip of Him will satisfy forever.

The Summons to All

On another occasion, Jesus issued a similar invitation when He said: 'Come to Me, all who are weary and heavy-laden, and I will give you rest. Take My yoke upon you and learn from Me, for I am gentle and humble in heart, and YOU WILL FIND REST FOR YOUR SOULS. For My yoke is easy and My burden is light' (Matt. 11:28-30). This summons requires that the one who comes to Christ must humble himself and come under His yoke. Our Lord is speaking with metaphorical language. As an ox would submit to the yoke of its master, one must come to Christ and yield to His lordship.

By this gospel invitation, Jesus called for those in the crowd to exchange their heavy load of sin for His light yoke of grace. Jesus was offering true rest for their weary souls. Even so, He calls you to cease from your labors to earn salvation. Stop your tireless efforts of self-righteousness. Come and rest in His saving work on your behalf.

The one who issues the call sets the terms. No one comes to Jesus on his or her own conditions. No one cuts their own deal with Christ. No one negotiates lower terms with the Master. There is no give and take between these two parties. The terms may only be accepted or refused—but never altered. This requirement is fixed by Jesus Himself.

The Hate Jesus Loves

To the astonishment of the crowd, Jesus set the conditions shockingly high. Christ emphatically states that if anyone comes to Him, he must hate those whom he loves the most. This word *hate* leaps off the page every time we read this. It is a word that sounds harsh and offensive. This undoubtedly jolted those who first heard this. These provocative words demand careful attention. Quite frankly, these words are too strong to be ignored.

By this stunning statement, Jesus addressed those personal relationships that are the most cherished. He spoke to those human bonds of affection where the deepest loyalties lie. He started closest to home. He began with the family members who meant the most to them—their parents, spouse, children, and siblings. 'If anyone comes to Me and does not hate his own father and mother and wife and children and brothers and sisters, he cannot be My disciple.' What did Jesus mean?

An Intentional Exaggeration

As Jesus speaks, He is using a figure of speech known as hyperbole. This is an exaggerated statement that is intended to provoke thinking and make a critical point. In this case, Jesus is deliberately setting love and hate in contrast to each other. He places them in juxtaposition as polar opposites. When Jesus says we must 'hate' our own family members, He actually means we must love them less than we love Him. He indicates that anyone who would follow Him must love Him more than the people closest to them. We must love Him more than anyone or anything in this world. If we are to be a true disciple of Christ, what we feel for others must appear to be as hate when compared to the greater devotion that we have for Him.

Scripture Interprets Scripture

This understanding is confirmed when we use Scripture to interpret Scripture. Jesus Christ Himself clarifies this perplexing statement elsewhere when He stated, 'He who loves father or mother more than Me is not worthy of Me; and he who loves son or daughter more than Me is not worthy of Me' (Matt. 10:37). Here, the words of Christ become crystal clear. We must love Jesus *more than* all others. This requires the commitment of one's entire life to Him. There can be no rival affections that compete with our surpassing love for Christ.

If we are to follow Christ, He must be our first priority and our foremost passion. Jesus will not settle for second place in any life. He says, 'Seek first His kingdom and His righteousness' (Matt. 6:33). Everything else in life is peripheral—Jesus is primary.

Mind, Affections, and Will

Loving Jesus Christ begins with our *minds*. We cannot love someone we do not know. We cannot love another person until we know something about them. Loving Christ begins with knowing who He is. What His character is. What He has done, is doing, and will do. We must learn what He said and taught. In order to love Jesus Christ, our minds must be filled with the true knowledge of Him. Love for Christ can never be cultivated in an intellectual vacuum. All love for Him starts with gaining a deeper knowledge about Him.

Further, love for Jesus Christ also requires strong *affections* for Him. Our knowledge about Christ should stoke the flames of deep feelings for Him. As we learn about the person and work of the Lord Jesus Christ, our hearts should be enflamed with fervent desire for Him. How could they not be? Beholding the perfect holiness of Christ and observing His sacrificial love at the cross should melt our hearts. No genuine follower of Christ can look at His sinless life and His saving work and be unmoved. Our relationship with Him should never be cold, never clinical nor stoic. There has to be a fervent first-love for Christ that ignites our souls for Him.

Finally, any genuine love for Christ will also direct our *wills*. Jesus said, 'If you love Me, you will keep My commandments' (John 14:15). This means our love for Christ should produce obedience to Him. Where genuine love for Christ is the root, grace-fueled obedience will be the fruit.

A Full Commitment

For example, marriage is a good illustration of this. When I met my wife Anne, we initially got to know each other on an intellectual level. I first acquired an understanding of who she is and what she likes. I learned about her life priorities, goals, and ambitions. There was a distinctly intellectual component in learning about her background and interests. Next, an excitement level soon arose in my heart for her. I was emotionally drawn to be with her. These feelings grew more and more. The depth of my affections for her compelled me to ask her to marry me. I pledged my life to her. As I stood at the front of the church at our wedding, I chose to commit myself to her for the rest of my life.

This is a faint picture of what it is like to become a follower of Christ. It means that you come to know about Him. But you do more than merely know who He is and why He came. It means that you love and adore Him. Then, you choose to devote your life to Him.

Hating Your Life

Jesus followed with another provocative statement about following Him. With His next statement, His words revealed a yet deeper level of what is required to follow Him. Christ also added that each person must hate 'even his own life' (v. 26). These words mandate that you must love Christ far more than you even care for your own life. A follower of Christ must die to self-love. You cannot remain self-absorbed, self-willed, and self-reliant *and* live for Him. You must love Him more than you love yourself.

Jesus then issues this strong warning, 'or you cannot be My disciple.' A genuine follower of Jesus Christ cannot love himself supremely. For any authentic disciple, Christ must be the number one affection. This is the supreme loyalty that He demands. The greatest allegiance of any follower's life must be the Lord Jesus. This level of commitment is non-negotiable. It is absolutely necessary in order to be His disciple. Jesus does not want a mere place in our lives. He commands the preeminence.

Non-Negotiable Terms

It is easy to merely linger in the crowd, tagging along behind Him. It is easy to be caught up in the high emotions of the multitude. But when Jesus addressed the crowd, He called for what is most difficult—the total surrender of each person's life. Otherwise, they cannot be His disciples. Jesus stated this in the negative so that His words will have a sharp edge to them. He meant to grab their attention and provoke their thinking.

To this day, Jesus continues to call individuals to Himself. This same demand remains unchanging today. He is calling you to love Him more than your own father and mother. The Lord issues you this summons to love Him more than your brother and sister. He is inviting you to have a greater love for Him than for your own life.

Have you answered this invitation? Have you come to Christ by faith? If not, do so now.

No Fine Print

And He turned and said to them, 'If anyone comes to Me, and does not hate his own father and mother and wife and children and brothers and sisters, yes, and even his own life, he cannot be My disciple'
(Luke 14:25-26).

One thing was certain about the invitation Jesus issued to this crowd—there was no fine print in the terms. He did not hide the cost required in following Him. He never marked down the price tag. He never lowered the terms. He never dumbed down the message. He never tried to induce a shallow decision. He never lowered the requirement to follow Him.

Large crowds were never His goal. Making true disciples was His aim.

Jesus made the high cost of following Him clearly known. He announced on the front end what it would require. He let it be known to all His listeners what the price was.

How different this is from the way religious hucksters work. Charlatans are smooth-talking conmen. They are shell game specialists. Sleight-of-hand magicians with words. They induce people to buy their message by bypassing what Jesus said is the true cost. They keep the high price of being a disciple hidden. They focus, instead, upon the perks. They exaggerate what their hearers will gain. But they never tell them what they must sacrifice. They avoid presenting the full price of a personal commitment to Christ.

Tragically, this is why so many people presume following Jesus Christ is a stroll down an easy street. They hear about only the benefits of forgiveness of sin. To them, Jesus is an ever-present genie in a bottle. Always on call. Always ready to grant them three wishes. They fixate on a crown in heaven, without a cross on the earth.

A Full Disclosure

But not Jesus. He was a frank, forthright truth-teller. He gave a full disclosure of what following Him would cost. He was upfront with people. He understood that a genuine commitment requires people knowing what it will cost them. This is why He spoke about the personal sacrifice required. He challenged them on the front end with the demands of discipleship.

Tragically, many individuals today give no thought to what it will cost them to follow Jesus. It should come as no surprise to us that difficulty accompanies the gospel.

Consider what it cost Jesus to purchase our salvation. It will come at a high price for all who receive it. There was a cross for Jesus—and there will be a cross for us. We must never become disillusioned when we suffer for our loyalty to Christ. Nothing has failed. Sure, we want the benefits from Him. Certainly, we want the provision and protection He gives. But we must not forget what it costs to be His disciple.

What Is a Disciple?

At this point, an important question needs to be raised—what is a disciple? The word disciple is a term used three times by Jesus in these few verses. It is the last word in verses 26, 27, and 33. The full reality of becoming a disciple is the central thrust of this discourse. Jesus wanted His followers to be His fully devoted disciples. He was never interested in merely attracting curiosity seekers to enlarge the crowd. He did not want to gather people who were simply highly interested observers of His ministry. Rather, He demanded fully-surrendered followers. He desired only those who submitted their entire beings to Him. Before Jesus ascended back to heaven, He commanded His disciples: 'Go, therefore, and make disciples of all the nations' (Matt. 28:19). In this charge, He stressed that He was seeking disciples—not empty decisions, passive spectators nor fickle followers.

It would not be until years later that the early disciples were first called 'Christians' (Acts 11:26). Christian is the diminutive form for Christ, meaning a 'little Christ.' It was first a term of derision, intended to mock the early believers.

By this name, these initial followers of Christ were being belittled for their connection with Him—a crucified Jew considered to be public enemy number one. But these first believers embraced this association with their Master. They instead wore the name 'Christian' as a badge of honor.

However, during the earthly ministry of Christ, these early believers were first called disciples by Jesus Himself. A genuine disciple was a true believer in Jesus Christ. Today, the term disciple has come to mean something less. Unfortunately, it has been stripped of its original meaning. Presently, the word has been downgraded to represent anyone who attends a small group Bible study. Or someone who has a higher level of commitment. But as it was used by Jesus, the word disciple meant an authentic believer who was surrendered to Him with an obedient faith.

Under the Master
Given the importance assigned to being a disciple, it is critical that we know what the word means. It comes from a Greek word (*mathetes*) which means a learner or pupil. It was one who sat under the direct instruction of a master teacher. In ancient times, a rabbi—meaning teacher—was often an itinerant instructor who was followed by a small band of disciples. These students embraced his teaching and emulated his life. The rabbi would give his philosophy on life and teach on a broad range of topics. His followers would listen and adopt their rabbi's manner of thinking. It was common to see such mobile classrooms in active session in the streets of the cities.

A disciple of Jesus Christ is one who has submitted his entire life to Christ and lives in obedience to His teaching. In His earthly ministry, Jesus was often called rabbi, and His followers were His disciples. Being addressed as 'rabbi' (John 1:38, 49; 3:2; 4:32; 6:25; 9:2; 11:8) meant that He was recognized to be an authoritative teacher. His disciples chose to recognize the authority of His teaching and live out what He taught. Wherever Jesus went, He was surrounded by those who sat under His teaching.

During His days here, Jesus established a teacher-student relationship with those who followed Him. In simplest terms, a disciple was a learner and follower of Christ. He learned what Jesus taught and obeyed what he learned. This person obeyed His teaching—without active obedience, no one could be a true disciple.

Divine Truth Teacher

Throughout His ministry, Jesus claimed that His teaching was authoritative. He taught what He had directly received from His Father. He asserted: 'My teaching is not Mine, but His who sent Me' (John 7:16). That is, His teaching came with the divine authority of God Himself. Consequently, obedience to His teaching was direct obedience to God. Again He maintained: 'He who sent Me is true; and the things which I heard from Him, those I speak to the world...I do nothing on My own initiative, but I speak these things as the Father taught Me' (John 8:26, 28). Therefore, following what Jesus taught was actually obeying what God taught. Jesus affirmed: 'I speak the things which I have seen with My Father' (John 8:38). What Jesus received from God the Father, He taught His disciples.

Repeatedly, Jesus claimed solidarity between what God had taught Him and what He taught His disciples. 'For I did not speak on My own initiative, but the Father Himself who sent Me has given Me a commandment *as to* what to say and what to speak. I know that His commandment is eternal life; therefore the things I speak, I speak just as the Father has told Me' (John 12:49-50).

God Speaking

Again Jesus claims: 'The words that I say to you I do not speak on My own initiative, but the Father abiding in Me does His works' (John 14:10b). Jesus maintained that every truth He spoke was from the Father. Further, 'the word which you hear is not Mine, but the Father's who sent Me' (John 14:24b). A disciple receives the authoritative truth of God in the words of Christ.

A disciple of Christ recognized that His teaching was not merely one more voice amid the many religious teachers in the world. Rather, a true disciple realized that Jesus spoke the unparalleled wisdom of God. Whatever Jesus stated must be received as the final Word from God. A disciple recognized that Jesus's teaching is the highest authority and final arbitrator on every matter. Whatever Jesus said is in reality, the way things truly are. A disciple recognized the lordship of Christ and aligned his life under His teaching.

Teaching with Divine Authority

Being the Son of God, Jesus taught with divine authority. Consequently, those who heard Jesus 'were amazed at His teaching; for He was teaching them as one having authority, and not as their scribes' (Matt. 7:28-9). The crowds who gathered around Him were 'astonished' and said, 'Where did this man get this wisdom?' (Matt. 13:54). All who heard Jesus recognized the profundity of His teaching.

The whole crowd was 'astonished at His teaching' (Mark 11:18). This means that His teaching blew their minds, so to speak. Even those who were sent to arrest Him returned empty-handed, mesmerized by His words, saying, 'Never has a man spoken the way this man speaks' (John 7:46). Jesus exceeded any teaching they had ever heard. Again we read: 'They were astonished at His teaching' (Matt. 22:33). A genuine disciple was amazed at the teaching of Jesus Christ and chose to follow Him.

A Learner Who Follows

Jesus made it clear that His true disciples are marked by keeping His word. He declared: 'Not everyone who says to Me, "Lord, Lord," will enter the kingdom of heaven, but he who does the will of My Father who is in heaven will enter' (Matt. 7:21). His genuine followers are those who live in obedience to the teaching of God. Jesus asked, 'Why do you call Me, "Lord, Lord," and do not do what I say?' (Luke 6:46). This rhetorical question implies a negative answer. Those who genuinely confess Jesus to be their Lord will show the validity of their claim by their obedience. It was not the perfection of their lives, but its direction, that was distinct.

Jesus emphatically said: 'If you continue in My word, then you are truly disciples of Mine' (John 8:31). True disciples are obedient to His word. But such obedience must come from a heart of love for Him. He said: 'If you love Me, you will keep My commandments.... He who has My commandments and keeps them is the one who loves Me' (John 14:15, 21a). A disciple of Christ is one who walks in obedience to keep His words out of love for Him.

The True Measure of Success

Unlike many today, Jesus Christ never measured the success of His ministry by the size of the crowd. He knew full well how easy it was to attract swelling numbers of empty followers. Jesus knew that one could remain inconspicuous in the crowd without making a genuine commitment to Him. He understood the magnetic pull of being drawn to a large group of people. Many people simply want to be wherever other people are—nothing more. The bigger the crowd, the more others will be present. But they can be present without making a real commitment.

To the contrary, the Lord desired a handful of genuine disciples. He wanted a few followers who walked in obedience over a large number of mere observers. He was interested in the spiritual reality of the individuals attached to Him, not the numerical size or external appearance of the crowd.

A Discerning Gaze

Because of the superficiality of the crowd, Jesus did something that shocked His twelve disciples. He sized up the crowd and knew it had become a mixed bag of people. They were at different places, spiritually speaking. Some were committed. Many were uncommitted. He saw that many—if not most—were superficial attenders with no level of faith in Him. As a result, Jesus stopped and turned around to address this multitude. He realized that it was becoming far too easy to tag along with Him.

In what He said, the Lord makes known the necessary requirements for being a true disciple. Here are the bare minimum prerequisites to be His disciple. As Jesus issued these words, He called for the unconditional surrender of their lives to Him. Such humble submission is the hallmark of a genuine disciple.

Still Shocking Today

What Jesus said is still shocking to this day. The terms for following Him remain just as demanding as when He first spoke them. The high cost of being His disciple has never been lowered. Salvation is offered freely to all who will receive it. Jesus Christ paid in full the sin-debt of sinners at the cross. He promises His saving grace as a free gift to those who do not deserve it. But if you are to receive it, you must humble yourself under His supreme authority.

These words spoken by Christ negate any easy believism. No true disciple can live contrary to his confession of Christ. This requires that you must examine yourself. Are you a genuine follower of Christ? Have you surrendered your life to Christ? Jesus said, 'If anyone wishes to come after Me, he must deny himself, and take up his cross daily and follow Me' (Luke 9:23). There is no fine print here. To be a true disciple, you must step out of the crowd to follow Him.

Will you follow Jesus?

CROSS-BEARING

Whoever does not carry his own
cross and come after Me cannot be
My disciple (Luke 14:27).

Few statements that Jesus ever issued were more scandalous
than what He said next. In no uncertain terms, Jesus said
that anyone who would follow Him must carry his own
cross. The severity of these words are hard for the modern
mind to grasp. Such provocative teaching was intended to
arrest the attention of His listeners. No doubt, it did. These
shocking words must have jolted this carefree crowd.

A Roman cross was considered an obscenity to the
first-century world. It was a form of capital punishment

reserved for only the most despicable criminals against the Roman Empire. In the ancient world, a cross was the most dreaded form of public execution. A cross was so offensive that no Roman citizen was allowed to suffer this barbaric death. Death by crucifixion was a slow, torturous death that purposefully prolonged the agony.

Yet, Jesus said to this crowd that those who would follow Him must take up their cross. These sobering words shocked the sensibilities of those in the crowd. Christ meant to shock their thinking. He intended to penetrate their conscience. These stunning words are as follows: 'Whoever does not carry his own cross and come after Me cannot be My disciple' (Luke 14:27).

An Open Invitation

In this verse, Jesus extended the same invitation He had previously stated—only this time even more sobering. This demanding summons began with the open invitation, 'whoever.' This all-inclusive 'whoever' parallels the 'anyone' in the preceding verse. No matter who they were, or whatever they had done, they were invited by Jesus to respond to this appeal. 'Whoever' is wide enough to include anyone in the crowd. This open appeal was extended to all in this vast multitude that day. Regardless of their social background, no matter what their moral failures had been, all were invited by this summons to follow Him. By saying 'whoever,' Jesus swung wide open the door leading into the kingdom of God. The gates of paradise were unlocked to allow all who would come to gain entrance.

This same open invitation had been extended by Jesus many times. Earlier, He said: 'Enter by the narrow gate' (Matt. 7:13). This invitation is broad in its scope. All who hear it should come at once. It does not matter how far removed a person's life may be from God. All are invited by Christ to come to Him. In His own day, Jesus was criticized for associating with sinners. His critics complained, 'This man receives sinners' (Luke 15:2). Yet Jesus said: 'the one who comes to Me I will certainly not cast out' (John 6:37). He also said, 'If anyone is thirsty, let Him come to Me and drink' (John 7:37). It did not matter how far short a person's life had fallen from what God required it to be. Jesus invited them to come.

The same is true today. It does not matter where you come from in life. It does not matter how sinful you have lived. It does not matter how offensive to God your life may be. Jesus is the Great Physician of the soul. He has not come into the world for those who are well. He has come for the sick. Your sin is no hindrance for Him to receive you.

The Terms of Acceptance

While extending this open invitation, Jesus set the narrow conditions for following Him. Jesus said: 'whoever does not carry his own cross...cannot be My disciple.' This statement contains a double negative. Twice in this one verse Jesus says 'not.' This makes His words doubly pointed and especially emphatic. Cross-bearing is mandatory for all who would answer this invitation. Anyone who follows Christ must carry his or her own cross. By these words, Jesus was not talking about wearing a piece of gold jewelry around one's neck. No one in the crowd would have misunderstood it that way.

In the first century, the cross was an instrument that inflicted the cruelest death. It was the most feared form of capital punishment in that day. The cross was the equivalent of the electric chair or deadly gas chamber in the ancient world. It meant a horrific death that unleashed the most excruciating pain possible. Death by crucifixion was so inhumane that it was reserved for the worst criminals. Only terrorists, insurrectionists, anarchists, robbers, thieves were hung upon crosses.

The Death March

The proceedings would unfold as follows. An accused criminal would stand trial before a judge, who had the power of life and death in his hands. If the accused was found guilty of a capital crime, he would be sentenced to death by crucifixion. The criminal would be forced to carry his crossbar through the streets of the city to the execution site on the outskirts of town. This was known as the dreaded death march. It was a public display of his guilt before the watching world. It was intended to heap great shame on the condemned. Carrying one's cross was a forced admission of guilt under the law—an agreement with the verdict of the higher court.

As the criminal carried his crossbeam, the people of the city would line both sides of the streets. This was meant to be a public spectacle. It signified that this offender was condemned by Rome and worthy of death. This despised individual was considered to be a dead man walking. It would be upon the criminal's crossbeam that he would be nailed and lifted up to die.

A Necessary Requirement

By this humiliating death march, Jesus is stating that those who follow Him must assume the very same posture, spiritually speaking. They must see themselves as having stood before the judgment of God, and been found guilty of breaking His moral Law. They have been weighed in the balances and found to be wanting. This means they agree with the divine verdict of the heavenly court.

Those who would follow Christ must see themselves in great need of God's grace. They must turn to Jesus Christ in repentance and faith to enter the kingdom. As a believer, they must carry their cross daily. This means that the ones who would follow Christ must not rely on themselves, but solely on Him. They must be continually looking to Jesus for strength and direction.

Coming After Jesus

When Jesus invited the crowd to come *after* Him, He was not talking in literal terms. As stated in the first chapter, He was not requiring that they take physical steps along the dusty road He was walking. Jesus is speaking in metaphorical terms. Individuals must take a decisive step of faith within their hearts. He called them to come after Him by their faith, not with their feet.

By this analogy, cross-bearing represented their personal allegiance to Christ. If anyone is to follow Him, they must carry their cross in this world. This means they must follow

Him in the manner that He prescribes. Jesus will not follow them. Instead, they must follow Him. That is, He will not do what they demand. Instead, they must do what He commands.

The same is true for everyone today. Cross-bearing is necessary for every person who would come after Christ. No one can follow Jesus *and* continue to live in their former manner of life. To follow Christ means you must make a complete turnaround. You must change the direction you were once traveling. Before you chose to follow Christ, you were walking away from Him—according to the course of this world (Eph. 2:3). You were headed toward destruction. To follow Christ, you must go in an entirely different direction. You must carry your cross and come after Him.

An Urgent Appeal

As Jesus extended this invitation, He did so in an urgent manner. Jesus was not casual or laid back about this appeal. He was not lackadaisical in His call. He did not adopt a take it or leave it attitude. Instead, He pressed upon them that they must respond to His invitation now. This was not something that could be delayed. This was a decision they could not postpone. They were not given the latitude to address other concerns first. They were not extended the option to pursue other interests over this one. This was the most important decision before them. It had to be answered immediately.

Responding to this invitation is the priority for every person. This call cannot be put off. It cannot be moved down your list of pressing matters. Answering this invitation is the single most important issue in your life. It must be answered now.

Now Is the Time

The Bible speaks to the urgency of choosing to take up your cross and carrying it now. The apostle Paul writes, 'Behold, now is "THE ACCEPTABLE TIME" behold, now is "THE DAY OF SALVATION"' (2 Cor. 6:2). The word 'now' indicates the pressing urgency in coming to Christ. Delaying a response to this invitation is a serious matter. The Bible says: 'Do not boast about tomorrow, For you do not know what a day may bring forth' (Prov. 27:1). Waiting to make a decision for Christ is a soul-endangering postponement. You have no idea if you will have time tomorrow to make this decision.

A Lifelong Decision

The decision to carry your cross is the one you must make. If you decide not to decide, that is a decision not to follow Christ. Your decision to carry your cross means death to your old way of life. It marks the beginning of an entirely new way of life. You must carry your cross every step of life's journey for the rest of your life. To carry your cross is not a one-time act, reserved for the beginning of following Christ. Cross-bearing must be a daily experience and will continue the entirety of your life.

If you are to follow Christ, you must step out of the crowd. You must turn your back on the world. You must travel down this new path. You must be willing to go wherever Jesus sends you. You must do whatever He calls you to do. Or you cannot be His disciple.

These are strong words. But strong words make strong disciples, who have strong faith.

Following Jesus (I)

Whoever does not carry his own
cross and come after Me cannot be
My disciple (Luke 14:27).

The greatest invitation ever issued is extended by Jesus in
the gospel. It is an open appeal to all who hear His voice
to come to Him. Jesus issued many such appeals to crowds
throughout His public ministry. He repeatedly called people
to come and commit their lives to Him.

Among these many summons, the most frequently given
one was the call to follow Him. Thirteen times in the four
Gospels we read these words 'Follow Me.' This is exactly what

Jesus is saying through this call. When He invites this crowd to 'come after Me,' He is saying 'Follow Me.'

By this appeal, Jesus was not enlisting people to join a social cause. Nor was He recruiting individuals to a religious movement. He was not signing up people to a political group. The invitation issued by Jesus was a call to follow Him in a personal, spiritual relationship.

Let us consider the various aspects of this powerful call. To answer it requires a commitment to Jesus Christ. What kind of resolve is needed? I want to designate six aspects of this commitment that are stated or implied in this call. In the next chapter, we will consider six more marks.

A Priority Commitment

First, Jesus was calling each person to follow Him *preeminently*. No other call that they would ever hear would take precedence over this one. Answering this invitation was the number one priority in their life. This call stood at the head of the list for what was most critical for them. Nothing could overshadow this call. Answering this call would be the most important decision of their life.

The significance of this appeal was found in the One who was issuing the call—the Lord Jesus Christ. Summoning them was the One sent to rescue them from the wrath to come. Voicing this call was the One validated by God as the Messiah sent to deliver them from their sins. This One speaking had restored sight to the blind. Hearing to the deaf. Limbs to the lame. Health to the sick. Life to the dead. Peace over the raging storms. They must respond to Him.

The same is true for you. The call of Jesus upon your life remains the most important issue confronting you. Nothing takes precedence over this summons. Answering it is the top priority in your life.

A Personal Commitment

Second, Jesus was calling each person to follow Him *personally*. Each person was required to make this decision for themselves. No one else could respond for them. Their spouse could not answer it for them. Their friends could not respond on their behalf. Though they were a large multitude, this could not be answered by a group vote. Jesus was requiring that each individual person respond to this truth. Each person had to exercise their own will. He was calling for a personal response, not a collective one.

Earlier, Jesus had asserted: 'Enter through the narrow gate' (Matt. 7:13). This gate represents Jesus Himself (John 10:7) and the conversion that leads into the kingdom of God. This gate is so constricted that it prohibits an entire group of people to pass through it. There is room for only one person at a time to pass through its tight confines. Everyone who comes to Christ must come to Him individually.

This is the personal decision that you must make to follow Christ. No one else can make this commitment for you. Your husband or wife cannot do this for you. This is not even a decision that your pastor or spiritual mentor can make for you. This must be *your* choice to follow Christ. This requires the exercise of *your* will. You must own this relationship with Christ.

A Repentant Commitment

Third, Jesus called those in this multitude to follow Him *repentantly*. Those in the crowd could no longer walk as they once did. They had to do a reverse pivot. They had to turn their backs to the practice of sin. They had to forsake their old ways of life. They could no longer live for themselves. They could no longer run after the sin they once pursued. They must renounce the self-centered focus by which they had been previously operating. They must exit the broad path of the world if they are to enter the narrow gate.

The call that Jesus issued was a command to repentance. Jesus began His public ministry by saying: 'Repent, for the kingdom of heaven is at hand' (Matt. 4:17). He announced: 'Repent and believe in the gospel' (Mark 1:15). In order to follow Jesus, there had to be repentance—a godly sorrow over one's own sin and the turning away from it.

Repentance is absolutely necessary to follow Jesus. He is the holy, sinless Son of God. He has never walked in sin nor pursued unholy pleasures. Those whom He calls to follow Him must turn their backs on the evil world's system. They must set their faces toward Jesus and the pursuit of personal holiness. No one can follow Christ without abandoning their former lifestyle in sin.

Those unconverted in this large crowd were traveling the broad path. This spacious path was, in essence, wide enough to accommodate their sinful lifestyles. This expansive highway could permit any manner of living they chose. It could tolerate any standard of morality they desired. But to follow Christ, they must exit this large path and enter the narrow path that leads to eternal life. This is the repentance that Jesus demanded.

This requirement of renouncing sin remains the same today. This necessity of turning away from living in sin remains in effect. Following Christ necessitates that you turn away from the sinful path you once traveled. Coming after Jesus means that you walk away from your sinful past. It requires that you travel down an entirely new path of following Jesus in a sanctified life.

A Trusting Commitment

Fourth, Jesus was calling them to follow Him *believingly*. That is to say, this decision to follow Christ necessitated that they come to personal faith in Him. When Jesus issued this call, He did not tell them where this path would take them. Neither did He explain everything that would be required. He did not reveal who else would be joining them. Whether the whole crowd would come, or no one else would come, their singular responsibility was to follow Him by faith.

This call required that they trust Jesus for everything. This begins by looking to Him for salvation. By this commitment, they rely upon Him solely for a right standing before God. They must be dependent upon Him to deliver them from the wrath of God which they deserve. They must believe in Him to rescue them from the just punishment for their sins. They must attach themselves to Him to receive His forgiveness and righteousness.

A Wholehearted Commitment

Fifth, Jesus called those in the crowd to come after Him *wholeheartedly*. To answer this call, these individuals had to step out of the crowd and fully align themselves with Him. They could not hold back any secret part of their life from Him. They could not be half in, and half out. They could not come to Him and still remain with the crowd. Their entire life must be surrendered to Him, or they could not be His disciples.

No one could follow Christ with a divided heart. Jesus addressed this wholehearted commitment when He said: 'No one can serve two masters; for either he will hate the one and love the other, or he will be devoted to one and despise the other. You cannot serve God and wealth' (Matt. 6:24). This meant that no one could be His true follower and remain consumed with this world. This call demanded an all or nothing response. No one could ride the fence. They could not play all ends into the middle. They must plant both feet onto this path.

Nothing Has Changed

Nothing has changed today. Jesus will not accept second place in your life. He demands the primary preeminence. Or He will not be a part. There cannot be a divided loyalty in your heart. You cannot follow Him *and* something else. You cannot follow Christ *and* pursue this world. You cannot love your family or job more than you love Him. You walk with Jesus *and* run after earthly pleasures. If you follow Him, Jesus must be your greatest passion and pursuit.

By this call, Jesus is demanding your total allegiance to Him. This mandates the unhindered response of your entire being. There must be a surrender of your entire life to Him. Is this where you are? Is this the kind of commitment you have made to Him? If we are to follow Jesus, we must be all in with Him. This is too important a decision to respond halfheartedly and play church.

An Unconditional Commitment

Sixth, Jesus called those in the crowd to follow Him *unconditionally*. He summoned them to follow Him no matter what it would require. No matter where it would take them. Jesus urged the multitude to come after Him without any further explanation. Regardless of what difficulties lay ahead, they must come after Him. Regardless of what affliction this would cost them. Regardless of what persecution awaited them.

There were no limits placed on their commitment. Whatever it would take to fulfill His will was what they must be willing to give. There could be no disciple who said to Christ, 'I will only go here to serve the Lord, but never there.' There could be no place off-limits where a follower of Christ would not be willing to advance. A follower has no power to veto. A believer could not set restrictions on what he would do for Christ.

In our day, you must have a similar unconditional trust in Jesus. You do not know where this journey will take you. Nor what it will require of you. You do not even know who will travel this path with you. Jesus does not provide us with details. He does not send His itinerary for your life. He makes no promise of an easy life. Your entire journey must be lived by trusting our new Master. And though you may not know the future or what it holds, you can trust our Savior who suffered on the cross to redeem lost sinners.

We must suffer any hardship for Him. We must be willing to go anywhere, do anything, and pay any price. He has paid the ultimate price on the cross. We must respond to this great love with our own sacrifice for Him.

Where It Begins

These six marks of coming after Christ define what a true commitment to Him involves. This call to follow Him requires that you personally choose to commit your life to Jesus Christ. No one else can do this for you. Such an individual choice necessitates our wholehearted commitment to Him. You cannot be half in and half out with Christ. This decision requires that you repent of your sins and turn away from pursuing a life of self and turn to Christ. You must do this unconditionally with no strings attached. No escape clauses in the fine print.

Are you ready to make this kind of commitment to Jesus Christ? Be assured, He is ready to receive you.

Following Jesus (II)

Whoever does not carry his own
cross and come after Me cannot be
My disciple (Luke 14:27).

The Christian life is all about following Jesus Christ. Being His disciple means living in a personal relationship with Him. It involves believing in Jesus. It requires following Him throughout your entire life. It includes worshiping and adoring Him. It means treasuring Him above all else. It involves serving Him with your entire being. Simply put, the Christian life is living for Christ.

Many confuse being a Christian with merely being in church. Or being part of a religious group. But being a follower of Christ runs far deeper. Christianity is not about joining a cause. Neither is it keeping a code of conduct. Being a Christian is living a life abandoned to Christ. This is the central truth that Jesus was establishing. Each individual must not be merely in a religious group. They must actually know Jesus.

This is what we desperately need to experience. We must know Jesus and become His disciple. This is a decision that can only take place in our hearts. From this personal relationship with Christ flows a great love for Him and desire to worship Him.

In this chapter we will continue what we began to examine in the previous chapter. We have already noted the first six aspects of how we must follow Christ: preeminently, personally, repentantly, believingly, wholeheartedly and comprehensively. Here are six more distinguishing marks of following Christ. Let us now consider each one, beginning with the seventh mark.

An Obedient Commitment

Seventh, this call issued by Jesus required the crowd to follow Him *obediently*. This means that they were to live their lives in obedience to His Word. The words 'follow Me' are in the imperative mood and given as a command. This call is a gospel invitation. A free offer to be accepted or rejected. But it is more than that. It is also a command that must be obeyed. All saving faith in Jesus is obedient faith. The moment you choose to follow Christ, you are responding with an initial step of obedience to the imperative to follow Him.

In the Gospel of John, we read that believing in Jesus and obeying Him are used synonymously: 'He who *believes* in the Son has eternal life; but he who does not *obey* the Son will not see life, but the wrath of God abides on him' (emphasis mine, John 3:36). In this verse, believing in Jesus and obeying Him cannot be separated. To believe in Him is to obey Him. Jesus said: 'Why do you call Me, "Lord, Lord," and do not do what I say?' (Luke 6:46). This rhetorical question implies a negative answer. No disciple will live in prolonged, habitual disobedience to His Word. Jesus also said: 'If you continue in My word, then you are truly disciples of Mine' (John 8:31). Wherever there is true faith in Christ, there will be a habitual lifestyle of obedience to His Word.

Slaves of Righteousness

One identifying mark of a true disciple is obedience to what God commands in His Word. God has given the Holy Spirit 'to those who obey Him' (Acts 5:32). The apostle Paul maintains that every person lives a lifestyle of obedience one way or another. Either to sin or to Jesus. He writes: 'Do you not know that when you present yourselves to someone as slaves for obedience, you are slaves of the one whom you obey, either of sin resulting in death, or of obedience resulting in righteousness? But thanks be to God that though you were slaves of sin, you became obedient from the heart to that form of teaching to which you were committed' (Rom. 6:16-17). The point is, everyone lives in obedience to his or her master. Either a person lives under the governing power of sin or under the grace of Jesus. You either obey Christ, as your loving and righteous master—or you obey sin, which enslaves you and brings death and destruction.

The Bible says that Jesus is the source of salvation to 'all those who obey Him' (Heb. 5:9). Those who submit to the authority of God's Word and keep it are those who are saved. Peter states that those who believe the gospel 'obey Jesus Christ' (1 Pet. 1:2). The Scripture also states: 'By this we know that we have come to know Him, if we keep His commandments' (1 John 2:3). Those who truly know God in a saving relationship are those who live in obedience to Him. Saving faith always begins with obedience: 'This is His commandment, that we believe in the name of His Son Jesus Christ' (1 John 3:23). For the true believer, 'His commandments are not burdensome' (1 John 5:2-3) because they are a delight to keep.

An Open Commitment

Eighth, the call of Jesus also necessitated that those in the crowd follow Him *openly*. They must live out their allegiance to Him before the watching eyes of this hostile world. They must give an open, public testimony of their loyalty to Him. Jesus made this clear: 'For whoever is ashamed of Me and My words in this adulterous and sinful generation, the Son of Man will also be ashamed of him when He comes in the glory of His Father with the holy angels' (Mark 8:38). In other words, you must unashamedly make known your relationship with Him. You must not conceal from the world that you are one of His disciples.

The apostle Paul announced: 'For I am not ashamed of the gospel, for it is the power of God for salvation to everyone who believes, to the Jew first and also to the Greek' (Rom. 1:16). By stating this with a negative, he is making a powerful statement of his desire to make an open testimony of the gospel. The apostle is saying that he is eager to publicly preach the gospel in Rome, the hardest city in the known world to gain a reception for this message. Nevertheless, this is what following Christ requires.

We must openly proclaim Him before all. We are to be 'speaking the truth in love' (Eph. 4:15). Also: 'Let your speech always be with grace, as though seasoned with salt' (Col. 4:6). We are called to be a faithful witness for Christ, with grace and patience toward unbelievers.

Such an open witness for Christ is required for each one of us who follow Christ. We cannot walk with Him and be silent about where our allegiance belongs. It is our responsibility to openly testify for Him. As God gives opportunities, we must tell others about Christ.

A Continual Commitment

Ninth, Jesus called those in the crowd to follow Him *continually*. When Christ stated 'come after Me,' it is in the present tense. This means that Jesus' disciples must follow Him constantly every moment of every day. This requires a daily lifestyle of coming after Him. This would not be reserved for only Sundays. They were not free to live otherwise throughout the week. There would never be one moment of the day, month, or year when they would not be following Him.

You must follow Jesus in good times and in bad times. In days of prosperity as well as in seasons of adversity. You must never take a day off from following Him. There is never a sabbatical from following Him. No matter who you are with. No matter where you find yourself. You are to be always living for Christ in season and out of season. When it is convenient and when it is inconvenient. When it is accepted and when it is not accepted.

Jesus said elsewhere that those who come after Him must do so 'daily' (Luke 9:23). A commitment to Christ is not a one time event, but an ongoing reality. This decision will lead to an every day, all day, ongoing lifestyle.

An Exclusive Commitment

Tenth, Jesus called those in the crowd to follow Him *exclusively*. That is to say, they must come after Him only. They could not follow Him *and* still be a part of the dead religion of Judaism. They could not follow Him *and* the mangled teaching of the Pharisees. They could not follow Him *and* the traditions of the scribes. They could not come after Him *and* any self-styled religion. They must follow Him and Him alone.

Jesus must be their sole source of truth. They cannot look to Him *and* to the wisdom of the world. They cannot come after Him *and* the ways of the Romans or the Greeks. They must follow the teaching of Jesus Christ exclusively. He is *the* way, *the* truth, and *the* life. He cannot be heard as just one more voice amid the many teachers competing for our attention. We must follow Jesus—and no one else.

A Permanent Commitment

Eleventh, those whom Jesus called were required to come after Him *permanently*. Making this decision meant that there was no turning back to their former ways. He was not calling for a short-term commitment. Not one that could be terminated down the road. Jesus did not ask for a momentary stroll with Him. He was calling for a long-term agreement. This must be a lifelong commitment that would guide their every step for the rest of their lives. Once the decision was made, they have burned their bridges behind them. Their allegiance would always be to Him.

Jesus said: 'No one, after putting his hand to the plow and looking back, is fit for the kingdom of God' (Luke 9:62). This statement means that no one could plow a straight furrow while looking backwards. They must remain with their shoulder to the plow, looking forward. In like manner, no one can be a disciple who is constantly second-guessing himself whether he made the right decision to follow Christ. You cannot move forward with a backward-looking gaze. A genuine disciple will not desire to return to their former life. Jesus stated that such a person is not fit for the kingdom of God. Not as long as he was holding on to his past life in sin.

The apostle Peter said that a false believer turns back to his former life of sin—but not a true disciple. He writes, 'It has happened to them according to the true proverb, "A dog returns to its own vomit," and "A sow, after washing, returns to wallowing in the mire"' (2 Pet. 2:22). A counterfeit disciple is pictured as a dog and pig, as he returns to his former lusts. But a believer is neither like a dog nor a pig— he is compared to a sheep. He has a new nature by which he keeps moving forward, following after Christ.

A prolonged commitment to follow Christ is required of every disciple. Once this decision is made, we cannot go back. There can be no reversal of our life pursuit. There can be no U-turn that would allow us to retreat to our former desires and sins. There is no ninety-day return policy for the cross we bear. Following Christ is a lifelong commitment. Chasing after Christ is not a short sprint, but a long marathon. Do you see the depth and duration of a commitment required to follow Jesus?

An Immediate Commitment

Twelfth, when Jesus called those within this crowd, they were to respond *immediately*. There was a pressing urgency about answering this invitation that very moment. Following Christ was not a decision that could be postponed. The need was now. Other matters would have to wait. Life was too short to defer this. Death was looming. Eternity was only a heartbeat away. This call must be answered straight away before it is too late.

The gospel call still demands an immediate response from you. Jesus said: 'While you have the Light, believe in the Light, so that you may become sons of Light' (John 12:36). There is a limited time for you to believe in Christ. You must respond while the light of the gospel is shining. The opportunity will not always be there. Whenever Jesus calls, there is an urgency to respond immediately.

Do Not Delay

Jesus is extending His call to you now. Do not delay to answer Him. He desires that you come to Him immediately. You must respond to His call while there is time. The day is soon approaching when you will have no more time.

Have you recognized your need to answer His call? Will you step out of the crowd and follow Him? Will you come to Him by faith? I urge you to do so now.

COUNTING THE COST

For which one of you, when he wants
to build a tower, does not first sit
down and calculate the cost to see if he
has enough to complete it? Otherwise,
when he has laid a foundation and is
not able to finish, all who observe it
begin to ridicule him, saying, 'This
man began to build and was not able to
finish' (Luke 14:28-30).

Anything worthwhile in life comes with a cost. There is
always a personal sacrifice required with gaining something
valuable. This is true whether it is succeeding in work,
enjoying marriage, advancing in sports, or excelling
with a musical instrument. Wherever there is the gain of
something meaningful, there is sacrifice.

Nowhere is this truer than in the matter of following
Jesus. Salvation is offered to us as a free gift. But receiving it
always comes at a high price. There are no exceptions to this

truth. Granted, the sacrifice required for our faith in Christ will differ from one person to the next. The price to be paid for following Christ is higher for some than for others. We are born into different families, in different places, and at different times in history. But there will always be a price to pay to come after Jesus.

Therefore, those in the crowd must count the cost of following Jesus *before* they make their commitment to Him. If not, they could make a superficial decision that would prove to be disingenuous. Taking this step is so important that Jesus says it calls for a sober calculation. No one should decide this on a whim. The stakes are too high. It requires too much of you.

Back-to-Back Parables

To establish this point, Jesus told the crowd two parables in consecutive order. A parable is an earthly story with a heavenly meaning. These two stories were given back-to-back in order to communicate the same basic point. These two parables fit perfectly together—they are the heads and tails of the same coin.

In the first parable, Jesus explained that if anyone in the crowd chooses to follow Him, they must first calculate the cost. What is this price? It will cost them everything. The second parable gives the other side of the coin. If they choose *not* to follow Christ, the result will be the same. It will still cost them everything. A failure to commit their lives to Him will cost them to suffer eternal destruction. Whether they commit their life to Him or whether they choose to reject Him, it will cost them *everything*.

Since these words were first issued, this price tag has never been reduced. These demanding terms remain the same for each person today. Where do you stand? This choice will affect your life for as long as you live. It will even determine your eternal destiny. Whatever your decision, be careful to count the cost.

A Probing Question

The first parable that Jesus told began by asking, 'For which one of you, when he wants to build a tower, does not first sit down and calculate the cost to see if he has enough to complete it?' (v. 28). When Jesus raised this question, He was looking squarely into the eyes of the individuals listening, with the intention of provoking their thinking. He sought to challenge them to honestly assess their relationship to Him.

By this probing question, Jesus was provoking them to undergo serious soul-searching regarding their spiritual state. Where are their hearts in relation to Him? Christ intended them to respond positively. But they must first count the cost of discipleship. He wanted to capture the attention of those who were merely curious about His notoriety. Jesus desired to secure the commitment of those who were simply caught up in the excitement of this movement.

Calculating the Cost

Jesus' illustration drew upon the common life experience of a builder on his construction site. Before starting a building project, any good builder would first count the cost of construction. A wise builder would never be so foolish as to begin to build without first calculating the total cost.

It would be short-sighted and ill-advised to rush into any construction project without, first, knowing what its total cost would be. The reason was simple enough. If the builder does not know the expense involved, he would discover it too late. He would soon realize that he was unable to complete this undertaking. He may be forced to abandon the project after wasting valuable time, money, and effort, to say nothing of his stained reputation.

In this parable, Jesus continued: 'Otherwise when he has laid a foundation, and is not able to finish all who observe it begin to ridicule him' (v. 29). What this builder started, he cannot finish. Why? Because he failed to estimate the cost on the front end. All started well. The ground had been prepared for construction. The trees were cleared out. The foundation was built up. The front door was set in place. The work was proceeding well. That is, until the project unexpectedly came to a standstill. No further building occurred. No more walls were erected. No more rooms were framed. No roof was laid over the structure.

As his neighbors walked past this unfinished project, they mocked him. They laughed at him. But it was not the laughter of humor. It was mocking derision. This foolish man had become a public spectacle before the eyes of the entire town.

The Foolish Builder

The observers of this unfinished project would have concluded, 'This foolish builder must have failed to do a cost estimate.' They rightly surmised that everything spent on this project was utterly wasted. Making it worse, everyone in town knew it. This imprudent builder was the object of scorn as the irresponsible man who started this building project, but was unable to finish.

How reckless it was for this builder to realize too late that the cost was too high. Sadly, he would lose everything he had invested into the project. How humiliating—even shameful—to walk away from this building project after he had started it. His only recourse would be to withdraw from the construction work. All was lost.

A Superficial Decision

This parable was directed at those in the crowd who were superficial followers of Christ. They had never counted the cost of what this would require from them. They were drawn in by the excitement of the crowd. They were attracted by the energy of the movement. They were interested in what Jesus taught about certain topics, but they never considered the ultimate cost and sacrifice. Consequently, they never made any real commitment to Him. How easy it was to jump onto this bandwagon and begin the journey. But how hard it would be to continue it, much less finish it. How effortless it was to launch this project. Yet how costly it would be to complete it.

Untold numbers of people are like this today. They appear to begin well in following Jesus. Maybe they start attending church. Perhaps they are inspired to get involved in a ministry. They are even moved by the hospitality being shown to them. All this makes them feel good. As a result, they make a hasty decision to repeat a prayer with a pastor. They join the church. They participate in a few spiritual meetings. They go through various religious motions. But, tragically, their apparent heart change is all external. They never genuinely come to know Jesus.

Abandoned Building Projects

Like the builder in the parable, this impetuous person appears to start well. Picture a single woman who begins to attend a local church. She participates in a Bible study. She makes new friends. She meets some persecution for her religious association. She is caught off-guard by this. She struggles with this rejection. She returns to her old friends, where she can be accepted. Old temptations return. Old sinful habits re-emerge. She falls back into her former way of life. Sadly, she never comes back to church. This woman is like this man in the parable who began to build, but was unable to finish. The cost to follow Christ was too high.

This parable represents a vast number of people today. They hear the truth about Jesus Christ. They want the benefits of salvation. They desire the peace of mind from knowing their sins are forgiven. They long for a home in heaven. But they give no thought to making a solid commitment to Christ. They are unwilling to give up the control of their life. So, when it comes down to making a decision, they walk away from following Christ.

Never Counted the Cost

Truth be told, this person was never a true disciple. They did not lose their salvation—they never had it. Though they gave the appearance of being a follower of Christ, they had never counted the true cost of being His disciple. They were never an authentic believer. The fact that they fall away from Christ reveals that they have never exercised true saving faith.

Any genuine devotion to Christ requires counting the cost before coming to Him. What will it cost you to follow Christ? It will cost you choosing to go your own way. It will cost you freedom to do your own thing. It will cost you a life of ease. It will require that you no longer live for yourself. You must burn your bridges behind you. There is no turning back.

It Will Cost You

What does it cost to be a disciple of Christ? It will cost you holding onto your self-righteousness. It will cost you cherishing your sin. It will cost you the control of your life. It will cost you the pursuit of the world.

You must count the cost of giving up your own views about life. You must count the cost of forsaking friendship with the world. You must acknowledge that you are no longer of the world. You must count the cost of foregoing your own plans for your life. You must be willing to follow God's will. You have to count the cost of letting go of your own will for His will.

Following Christ will cost you popularity with certain friends. It may cost you business success. It may cost you the applause of this world. Nothing in your life lies outside this commitment to Jesus Christ. You must think carefully about what this commitment requires. Otherwise, a rash decision to follow Christ may fizzle out before the finish. You must calculate this cost.

Be assured that the religion that costs nothing is worth nothing—and accomplishes nothing. Religion that costs you neither time nor thought, nor self-denial, nor sacrifice, nor prayer, nor suffering, nor opposition, nor persecution, nor conflict, will be a religion that will never save your soul. It is a religion that will give you no comfort in the day of adversity. It is a religion that will give you no peace in the day of your death.

More Gains Than Losses

Having issued this caution, let me remind you that what you gain far outweighs the losses. You give up your guilt and receive God's grace. You exchange your misery for His mercy. You substitute perishing in sin for His pardon from sin. You sacrifice the applause of men for the approbation of God. In reality, you gave up nothing—and you receive everything.

You do not know where following Jesus will take you. Neither do you know the specifics of what will be required of you. But you know *who* you are following and can trust Him through every circumstance. You can be fully confident in the Lord. Follow Him—no matter where, no matter what, no matter with whom.

If you will commit your life to Christ, you will gain far more than you give up. You will lose your old life, but you will gain a new, abundant life. You will lose this world, but you will gain a far better world to come. You will lose the passing pleasures of sin, but you will gain far better joys in Christ. The positives far outweigh the negatives.

This gracious invitation to follow Christ is extended to you. But before you answer, count the cost.

UNCONDITIONAL SURRENDER

Or what king, when he sets out to
meet another king in battle, will not
first sit down and consider whether
he is strong enough with ten thousand
men to encounter the one coming
against him with twenty thousand? Or
else, while the other is still far away,
he sends a delegation and asks for
terms of peace (Luke 14:31-32).

Following Jesus Christ demands the unconditional surrender of your life. If you are to be His disciple, you must submit to His supreme authority. You must recognize His right to rule over you. You must relinquish everything to Him. You must give up all personal rights. This yielding is necessary—it is non-negotiable.

In the crowd that day, there were those who were uninformed about the high price of following Christ. They were swept up in the buzz of the moment. They had no idea of the demands of Christ. They were clueless as to the dangerous condition in which they found themselves. Unknown to them, they were at war with this One whom they were following. Even more seriously, they were unaware that He was at war with them.

In this second parable, Jesus addressed this stark reality. Jesus illustrated the sober consequences of not following Him on His terms with the following story. This parable involved a military conflict between two adversarial kings. Each monarch has two marching armies at his command. These two rulers are in a state of war with each other. But the confrontation is a terrible mismatch. The approaching king leads vastly superior soldiers into this conflict. His dominant military strength will result in the sure defeat of the lesser king. This outmanned ruler must surrender to the advancing king before it is too late. As we study this parable, the application for our lives will be obvious.

When Two Kings War

Jesus began by setting the scene: 'Or what king, when he sets out to meet another king in battle' (v. 31). Here, He spoke of these two kings who are at war with each other. Each monarch reigned over his own kingdom. These two sovereigns were entering into battle with each other, leading their respective forces. There was a bitter opposition between them, and a building strife had escalated to a breaking point. They are two powers in intense conflict, involving each of their kingdoms. This rivalry was so intense that an inevitable battle was soon to occur.

In this heated clash, only one king will emerge victorious. These are not two equal powers. One ruler is far superior to the other. The stronger sovereign will easily gain the domination over his weaker foe. He will, in turn, gain the spoils of victory. The lesser king will lose everything and become the slave of the other. The one who suffers defeat will even lose his life. This is a winner-takes-all battle.

The Necessary Calculation

In this parable, Jesus further explains that when the inferior king realizes that he has no chance of victory against the superior monarch, he must 'first sit down and consider whether he is strong enough with ten thousand men to encounter the one coming against him with twenty thousand' (v. 31). This endangered king must consider what it will mean for him to enter into battle with this dominant despot. He must calculate whether his forces can withstand such an attack. He must weigh his chances against these advancing forces. The under-manned ruler must determine whether he is strong enough with half the soldiers to withstand the assault of this greater king.

The only rational conclusion is this: there is no way that the outnumbered king can prevail against the threat posed by the greater monarch. If he enters into this conflict, he will surely be defeated and destroyed. There is no possibility that the outmanned ruler can stand up to the ruthless aggression of the greater ruler. This short-handed king must come to his senses and soberly realize he is at a severe disadvantage. He must act immediately before it is too late.

The Confronted King

To properly understand this parable, these two powers need to be identified. As Jesus told this story to the immense crowd, both of these warring monarchs were standing there that day. The lesser king represented each fickle follower in the crowd that day. By this analogy, each person—much like a king—has the responsibility to preside over the affairs of his kingdom. An enthroned ruler reigns over the business of his domain. A ruler must think carefully about the issues confronting him. His decisions will affect the future of his kingdom.

So it was with each uncommitted person in the crowd. These superficial followers were like a king who ruled over a kingdom. In this case, they presided over the affairs of their own lives. The issue of following Christ necessitated their careful deliberation, like a ruler when presented with a crisis. What they decide concerning Jesus will not only affect their present conditions, but, ultimately, it will determine their eternal destiny. No decision will ever compare with the importance of this one.

The Approaching King

In this parable, the other king is the one who is telling this story. This approaching monarch is Jesus Christ Himself, who possesses infinitely greater power. He is the Almighty, the King of kings and Lord of lords (Rev. 19:16). He possesses and exercises absolute sovereignty over every living person. His authority is unrivaled. No foe can withstand His advances. He claims: 'All authority has been given to Me in heaven and on earth' (Matt. 28:18). Unrivaled authority belongs to Him alone.

Concerning this King, the Bible says: 'And to Him was given dominion, glory and a kingdom, that all the peoples, nations and men of every language might serve Him. His dominion is an everlasting dominion which will not pass away; And His kingdom is one which will not be destroyed' (Dan. 7:14). Paul maintained that God the Father 'raised [Christ] from the dead and seated Him at His right hand in the heavenly *places*, far above all rule and authority and power and dominion, and every name that is named, not only in this age but also in the one to come. And He put all things in subjection under His feet' (Eph. 1:20-22). This statement announces the unlimited sovereignty of Jesus Christ over all the universe. This includes every single person on earth.

Every human life is subjected beneath the omnipotence of Jesus Christ. Every person is subordinated to His decisions. Paul wrote: 'God highly exalted Him, and bestowed on Him the name which is above every name, so that at the name of Jesus EVERY KNEE WILL BOW, of those who are in heaven and on earth and under the earth, and that every tongue will confess that Jesus Christ is Lord, to the glory of God the Father' (Phil. 2:9-11). This statement reveals Jesus' exalted position over all heaven and earth.

The Conflict of the Ages

This parable teaches the hostile war that exists between sinful man and holy God. They are not at peace with each other, but are in heated conflict. The lesser king is at war with the greater king. This represents the spiritual enmity that every unconverted person has toward Jesus Christ. Those in the crowd that day did not realize the state of war in which they found themselves. But it is their unbelief that has placed them into this spiritual warfare against God. They were not in peacetime conditions with Him, but in a state of declared war.

The rest of the Bible confirms this truth. Every unbeliever finds himself in cosmic rebellion against heaven's King. Jesus said: 'He who is not with Me is against Me' (Matt. 12:30). Paul states that all unbelievers are 'enemies' of God (Rom. 5:10). Moreover, they are 'alienated and hostile in mind, engaged in evil deeds' (Col. 1:21). This is the spiritual treason of the human race against almighty God.

The Warring Christ
This parable, however, teaches something even more sobering. It pictures Jesus Christ at war with sinners who refuse to repent and surrender to Him. In speaking about 'the wrath to come,' John the Baptist warned that irreversible judgment was imminent: 'The axe is already laid at the root of the trees; therefore every tree that does not bear fruit is cut down and thrown into the fire' (Matt. 3:10). Jesus Christ Himself will be the Executer of this divine wrath against all unbelievers.

Jesus is the One who 'judges and wages war' (Rev. 19:11). Scripture says: 'And the armies which are in heaven, clothed in fine linen, white *and* clean, were following Him on white horses. From His mouth comes a sharp sword, so that with it He may strike down the nations, and He will rule them with a rod of iron; and He treads the wine press of the fierce wrath of God, the Almighty' (Rev. 19:14-15).

The application is unmistakable. Jesus issued this warning to those in the crowd. They were not in a neutral state with Him. There is no neutral state with Christ. You are either on His side or at war with Him. And yet He offers peace through His terms to all His enemies, but you must accept them in full. He extended grace to us in this invitation, but we must respond with our surrender because He is approaching in the final judgment. This is a hard truth, but truth nonetheless.

Terms of Peace

As this parable concludes, Jesus explained the mercy He offered to the crowd. It was found in the form of this superior king who offered terms of peace: 'Or else, while the other is still far away he sends a delegation and asks for terms of peace' (v. 32). The encroaching king with vastly superior forces offers terms of reconciliation. The only rational decision for the inferior king to make would be to surrender. If the outmanned king does not accept this truce, he will lose the battle. Any sane ruler would come to his senses and accept his offer of peace. This lesser king cannot withstand conflict with this greater king. This superior king is coming, but offers to end the war with his offer of peace.

In this parable, the terms of peace are found in the cross of the Lord Jesus Christ. It is Christ alone who makes peace between God and man. The Bible says: 'Therefore, having been justified by faith, we have peace with God through our Lord Jesus Christ' (Rom. 5:1). This peace is exclusively found in Jesus Christ, who is 'our peace' (Eph. 2:14). In His first coming the apostle Paul states: 'and He came and preached peace to you who were far away, and peace to those who were near' (Eph. 2:17). By His substitutionary death, Jesus 'made peace through the blood of His cross' (Col. 1:20). This is the free offer of 'the gospel of peace' (Eph. 6:15) to those under divine wrath. The good news is that God in Christ will forgive the offenses of His enemies, no matter how immense the sins are.

Unconditional Surrender

Jesus Christ extends to you His terms of peace. He will end the warfare between Him and you. This is the promise of full reconciliation. No right-thinking person will want to enter into conflict with Jesus Christ on the final day. You must respond to His invitation that requires your full surrender. You cannot cut your own deal with Him. He will not negotiate. The invitation is to accept His terms of peace. Jesus is calling for your verdict. Accept His offer before it is too late. Unconditionally surrender your life to Him.

UNDER NEW MANAGEMENT

So then, none of you can be My
disciple who does not give up all his
own possessions (Luke 14:33).

As Jesus sized up the crowd following Him, He rightly
assessed where they stood with Him. With penetrating
insight, He saw into their hearts. He concluded that
they needed to surrender their lives to Him. They yet
needed to come under His ruling authority. Everything
they were and everything they had must come under
His governing control.

This becomes clear in the next statement Jesus made:
'So then, none of you can be My disciple who does not

give up all his own possessions' (Luke 14:33). I want us to look carefully at this demanding statement. Once we understand its true meaning, its implications for our lives are staggering.

A Sharp Negative

Jesus began this part of His discourse with a strong negative. This was so that His sharp words would have a cutting edge to them. He maintained: 'None of you can be My disciple.' These blunt words are abrupt. It hardly seems the way to invite others to follow you. But this is exactly how Jesus issued this summons. His biting words were intended to jolt the crowd toward careful thinking and a proper assessment. He was saying that none of them could be His disciple unless the following condition was met.

By saying 'none of you can be My disciple,' Jesus was indicating that they could not continue going along with Him in an uncommitted manner. They could no longer be merely curious and certainly not cavalier. They must come to the point of personal commitment to Him.

Every disciple, Jesus said, must 'give up all his own possessions' (v. 33). What did our Lord mean by this statement? Is salvation for sale? Must forgiveness of sin be bought? Must we give away everything that we own?

Buying Salvation?

First, Jesus was *not* saying that those in the crowd must purchase their salvation. No amount of material assets can acquire a right standing before God. He was not meaning that they must liquidate their material assets in order to buy a ticket to heaven. He was not requiring that they must pay their fee into heaven. The entire Bible speaks with one voice in teaching that salvation is a free gift. Grace is offered without cost through the finished work of Jesus Christ upon the cross.

Beginning in the Old Testament, this was abundantly clear. The prophet states: 'Ho! Every one who thirsts, come to the waters; And you who have no money come, buy and eat. Come, buy wine and milk without money and without cost. "Why do you spend money for what is not bread, and your wages for what does not satisfy?"' (Isa.55:1-2). God is saying that salvation can never be purchased with money. It cannot be bartered for with one's wages. The forgiveness of sins is not up for bid. Redemption is not for sale. No amount of money could buy freedom from the slave market of sin. The debt incurred by sin against God is simply too great to be moved by any human resources.

The apostle Peter confirms this fact when he writes: 'you were not redeemed with perishable things like silver or gold from your futile way of life inherited from your forefathers, but with precious blood, as of a lamb unblemished and spotless, the *blood* of Christ' (1 Pet. 1:18-19). No person has enough gold or silver to purchase any acceptance with God. No amount of money can remove sin from the human soul. Grace alone, purchased by Jesus at the cross, is the only remedy.

Becoming Paupers?

Second, Jesus is *not* saying that those who would be His disciples must take a vow of poverty. He is not advocating becoming a pauper as the means to salvation or spirituality. Christ is not teaching that His followers must divest themselves of all worldly goods. Such a dispossession would be senseless and a poor stewardship of resources. If His disciples sold all they owned, then others would have to feed and clothe them. This would be a miserable witness to the world.

To the contrary, the Bible teaches that if a man does not care for the members of his own household, he is worse than an infidel (1 Tim. 5:8). This clearly implies that the head of the house has financial resources at his disposal. He must use them to care for his family. This indicates that the husband is a hard worker and a breadwinner. He acquires wealth to be used to feed and clothe his own family. It would be shameful if someone else had to provide for his own family because he gave away all his money.

Moreover, Christians have a moral responsibility to help a fellow believer who is in physical need. They use their riches to meet the needs of others: 'If a brother or sister is without clothing and in need of daily food, and one of you says to them, "Go in peace, be warmed and be filled," and yet you do not give them what is necessary for *their* body, what use is that?' (James 2:15-16). Again we read: 'But whoever has the world's goods, and sees his brother in need and closes his heart against him, how does the love of God abide in him?' (1 John 3:17). If a disciple fails to provide for the needs of another disciple, it calls into question his love for God.

Furthermore, Jesus told several parables that were based upon the banking industry. In these stories, Christ commended the possession, lending, and borrowing of money. The shrewd investing of resources is a virtue, not a vice. The apostle Paul adds that the love of money, not the possession of it, is the root of all evil (1 Tim. 6:10). Some of the most notable believers in the Bible were rich by the standards of their day. Such financially well-endowed men included Abraham, Job, Solomon, and Joseph of Arimathea.

Let us be clear, Jesus was not teaching that His followers must give away all their assets before they can enter into His kingdom. And we see that neither was He implying that one must buy the grace that only God gives. So what did Jesus mean?

Stewards, Not Owners

Instead, what Christ is teaching in this statement—'must give up all his own possessions'—is this: every disciple must recognize that they have come under His lordship. In so doing, they have come under new management. As His follower, he realizes that he is merely a steward of what Christ has placed into his hands. A steward is a house manager, who oversees the possessions of his master. However, he himself owns nothing. He manages the properties that belong to the head of the house. A steward merely acts on behalf of his master in handling his assets. He lives in his master's house and oversees his belongings. He uses them to conduct his lord's business. But ultimately, he himself owns nothing.

This is the point Jesus was making with the crowd. They must see themselves as stewards of what they have. Their money will remain in their own pocket. But it must now be recognized as belonging to God. They will no longer be the owner of what they have, but merely the trustee. Those who follow Christ become a manager of what has been entrusted to them. Earthly things must now be used for the greater glory of God. Earthly treasures can no longer be used for selfish purposes. They must be invested in what will further the work of the kingdom.

Let me make this personal. If you are to become a disciple of Christ, your entire life will no longer be your life. Your whole existence belongs to Him. Your time will no longer be your time. Instead, it will be His time to be used for His purposes. Your talents will no longer be your talents. Rather, they will become His and used for His purposes. Your treasure will no longer be your treasure, but simply entrusted to you for this brief time of your life. You must recognize that all that you have must be seen as His assets.

A Forbidden Love

A disciple must no longer love most things of this world. He must supremely love God. The Bible warns: 'Do not love the world nor the things in the world. If anyone loves the world, the love of the Father is not in him. For all that is in the world, the lust of the flesh and the lust of the eyes and the boastful pride of life, is not from the Father, but is from the world' (1 John 2:15-16). A disciple may use the things of this world, and even enjoy these things. But they must never capture and control his affections. Chief passions are reserved exclusively for God.

This is precisely what Jesus meant: 'Do not store up for yourselves treasures on earth, where moth and rust destroy, and where thieves break in and steal. But store up for yourselves treasures in heaven, where neither moth nor rust destroys, and where thieves do not break in or steal; for where your treasure is, there your heart will be also' (Matt. 6:19-21). A disciple does not live to accumulate possessions in this life. He invests what he has in eternal purposes. Jesus continued: 'No one can serve two masters; for either he will hate the one and love the other, or he will be devoted to one and despise the other. You cannot serve God and wealth' (Matt. 6:24). The Lord did not condemn the possession of wealth. Rather, he denounced serving money and putting your trust and security in it.

Obtaining Eternal Life

Jesus was once approached by a rich young ruler, who asked: 'Teacher, what good thing shall I do that I may obtain eternal life?' (Matt. 19:16). By this question, this successful individual expressed that he wanted to gain salvation. Yet at the same time, he wanted to live for the things in this world. He wanted to add Jesus to his life, while still living for this world.

Jesus responded: 'Why are you asking Me about what is good? There is only One who is good' (v. 17). This prosperous person was ignorant of whom he was addressing. Jesus was clarifying that He was more than a teacher. He was God in human flesh—truly God and truly man.

Keeping the Law

This young man failed to see the perfect holiness of Jesus. Therefore, he failed to see his own unholiness. So, Jesus used the Law to reveal this man's sin. He said to him: 'if you wish to enter into life, keep the commandments' (v. 17). Jesus was not saying that this young man could earn salvation through perfect obedience. Quite the opposite, He was showing that he actually could not do so.

This high-end over-achiever responded: 'Then he said to Him, "Which ones?" And Jesus responded, "You SHALL NOT COMMIT MURDER; You SHALL NOT COMMIT ADULTERY; You SHALL NOT STEAL; You SHALL NOT BEAR FALSE WITNESS; Honor YOUR FATHER AND MOTHER; and You SHALL LOVE YOUR NEIGHBOR AS YOURSELF"' (vv. 18-19). With these five commandments, Jesus gave this man the second tablet of the Law. This was the easier part of the commandments to keep. The young man confidently replied: 'All these things I have kept; what am I still lacking?' (v. 20). He was naively oblivious to his own sin.

Loving Money

In this encounter, Jesus saw into his heart and detected his all-consuming love of possessions. Jesus needed to dig deeper and expose his sin of covetousness. Christ saw that money was his idol. He said: 'If you wish to be complete, go *and* sell your possessions and give to *the* poor, and you will have treasure in heaven; and come, follow Me' (Matt. 19:21). Jesus was not saying that he could not possess money. Rather, He meant that money could not possess him.

This cost was too high for this rich man. 'But when the young man heard this statement, he went away grieving; for he was one who owned much property' (v. 22). This young ruler turned and walked away from Christ. He loved his earthly riches more than a spiritual inheritance. He refused to abandon his old master—money—in order to receive a new Master—Jesus Christ.

Making the Point

This is precisely the point that Jesus was making with these large crowds. If any of them were to become His disciple, they must come under new management. They must make Him their supreme love and loyalty in their lives. They must hold everything they have with an open hand. He must become their number one priority. They must love Christ more than the things in this world.

This is, likewise, what Jesus is saying to you. Christ offers salvation to you as a free gift. It must be received by faith alone. But true faith involves the complete surrender of your life to Christ. Saving faith is entrusting your entire being to Him.

Where Are You?

Have you come to this place? Do you see that salvation is not a reward to be earned? Instead, the grace of God is a free gift offered to you. Have you received this gift?

Following Jesus requires far more than merely being in a religious crowd. Being a disciple is an internal, personal reality. Coming to Christ requires surrendering your life to Him. It necessitates a commitment that encompasses every area of your life. Everything you are and everything you possess must come under His new management.

Have you taken this deliberate step of faith? If you come to Jesus with decisive faith, He is ready to receive you.

TASTELESS SALT

Therefore, salt is good; but if even
salt has become tasteless, with what
will it be seasoned? It is useless either
for the soil or for the manure pile; it
is thrown out (Luke 14:34-35a).

Those in the crowd following Jesus must have wondered
when He would lighten the message. This was a hard-hitting
address. They must have expected that at some point, Jesus
would soften His message. They must have anticipated that
Jesus would eventually scale down His demands. He will
surely tone it down, right?

Will Jesus lower the admission requirements to enter
the kingdom? Will He ease up on His call for radical
commitment? Will He meet them halfway?

The answer is no. Rather than lessening His demands, Jesus continued the provocative challenge of His words. Becoming a follower of Christ must never be the result of a shallow response. Due to the weighty significance of His message, Jesus further spoke sobering words of what true discipleship requires. The full magnitude of what He said must have struck them hard. His teaching was straightforward and piercing. His truth was arresting. His demands were non-negotiable. These words by Jesus hit them with the force of a category five hurricane. They were not hard to understand—just hard to swallow.

To this very day, what Christ says continues to have major implications for you. This message cannot be easily dismissed as being reserved exclusively for this first-century crowd. This truth cannot be avoided by relegating it to ancient times. Rather, these words are as demanding today as when they were first spoken. They apply as directly to you as when Jesus first uttered them. So, you must give your careful consideration to what they require—or suffer serious consequences.

A Positive Commodity

In this next verse, Jesus brought His exacting message to a dramatic conclusion. He introduced these words by stating a general truth from everyday life. He began: 'Therefore, salt is good' (v. 34). Everyone could understand this. All could agree with this. Salt is good because it preserves meat from spoiling. Salt flavors otherwise bland food. Salt cleanses what is unclean. Salt even possesses medical properties that heal an open wound.

A disciple, Jesus said, is likened to salt. He had made this comparison earlier in the Sermon on the Mount when He said to His disciples: 'You are the salt of the earth' (Matt. 5:13). All followers of Christ are the salt of the earth. By their presence in society, they are to bring a moral influence upon the world. They are to hinder the sinful corruption of the world. The penetrating impact of their personal holiness is to be a preventative force in their surroundings. Disciples are not to be the sugar of the earth, but salt. They are to sting the raw wounds of the world's immorality. They are to produce a cleansing effect upon those around them. These sanctifying influences are to be produced in following Christ.

Salt That Loses Its Savor

However, Jesus followed His initial statement with a stern warning: 'but even if salt has become tasteless, with what will it be seasoned?' (v. 34). Jesus was indicating that not all salt is genuine. Some salt initially appears to be real, but in reality, is not. Some background is necessary to understand this. In this part of the world, there was a salty, rock-like mineral that had gypsum mixed with it. This hybrid rock—half salt and half gypsum—was not real salt. It was an easy-to-mistake imitation. Upon closer scrutiny, this alternate stone would eventually show itself to be a counterfeit substitute for salt. This mineral looked like the real thing but when sampled, it did not taste like authentic salt. Though it appeared to be salt, it was not genuine.

By this metaphor, the Lord was making a critical point. He was contrasting a true disciple and a false one. The phony follower merely had an outward façade of being a genuine disciple. But in reality, he was not. He gave the outward appearance of being an authentic disciple. But internally, he was devoid of any authenticity.

Tasteless salt, Jesus said, had no use. Neither did uncommitted disciples. Those in the crowd with a divided heart were like this fake salt. They were not committed to Christ. Consequently, they possessed no moral influence upon the world. They were worthless to hold back the corrupting influences of evil. They did not add any zest and flavor to the lives of others. They are like salt that had become tasteless. Though giving the outward appearance of being a true disciple, they in reality, were not. Their superficial commitment betrayed a wholehearted loyalty to Christ.

Can It Be Restored?

Jesus then asked this rhetorical question concerning tasteless salt: 'With what will it be seasoned?' This was a pressing inquiry that implied a negative answer. The answer is so obvious that Jesus did not bother to answer it. This kind of counterfeit salt is good for nothing. Earlier in His ministry, Jesus asserted: 'If the salt has become tasteless, how can it be made salty again?' (Matt. 5:13). The same negative answer is assumed. Real salt cannot become unsalty. Neither can tasteless salt become true salt.

Many in the crowd appeared to be salt. But these were not genuinely converted to Him. They only had a thin veneer of religiosity. They looked spiritual when mixed in with this religious crowd. But, with a worldly crowd, their true nature would be revealed. When with a different throng, they would be easily squeezed into the mold of the world. They were not in danger of losing their salvation, because they did not possess it. The truth is, they had never been converted to Christ. In due time, their true spiritual colors would be revealed. Those in the crowd would soon lose what little saltiness they had and would be revealed as not being genuine salt.

Good for Nothing

Jesus followed this statement with biting sarcasm: 'It is useless either for the soul or for the manure pile' (v. 35). He was asserting that tasteless salt is good for nothing. Imitation salt is not even good to be thrown into the manure pile. In this day, they did not have the modern convenience of indoor plumbing. Consequently, human waste was collected in a clay pot and carried outside to be thrown onto a dung pile. The stench was repulsive to anyone's sensibilities. To impede the foul smell, salt was thrown onto the excrement. However, what only looks like salt has in actuality no capacity to curb this loathsome odor. Such fake salt was entirely useless to perform even this base function. This is how Jesus described the half-committed crowd. They were entirely useless to God to stem the foul odor of this sinful world.

Those not fully devoted to Jesus were like counterfeit salt that had lost its flavor. Such members of the multitude had zero benefit to the kingdom of God. Such a marginal person could make no positive contribution to the mission of Jesus Christ. This kind of person—half in, half out with Christ—had no eternal contribution to the purposes of God.

Such a crowd-follower was not a Christ-follower. This person had only a superficial attachment to Christ and the excitement surrounding Him. This person had not yet come to know Jesus personally.

A Call for Self-Examination

These words by Jesus Christ are a serious call for self-examination. An unexamined life is a dangerous life to live. Such a superficial life is the breeding ground for self-deception. This was true with the twelve disciples, even among those closest to the Lord Jesus. One of them—Judas—was tasteless salt. He was a false disciple. Though he had a close association to Jesus, he had no saving relationship with Him. He was religious, yet lost. There were other Judases in this religious crowd going along with Jesus. In the same way, many in the religious crowd today are not genuine followers of Christ.

The apostle Paul writes: 'Test yourselves to see if you are in the faith; examine yourselves!' (2 Cor. 13:5). Everyone who hears the Word of God should audit their own soul. You should ask yourself: am I genuinely converted to Christ? Do I see the evidence of a changed life? Have I sincerely called upon the name of the Lord for salvation? Do I have a living relationship with Jesus Christ?

Untold multitudes profess faith in Jesus, but do not truly know Him. Many are in church, but are not in Christ. Many are religious, but not regenerated.

Could this be true of you? Could you be clinging to an empty conversion experience that was not genuine? Could you lack the assurance of your salvation because you do not possess it?

If there is any doubt about where you are with the Lord, listen to these words of Jesus. The Bible also says: 'Seek the Lord while He may be found; Call upon Him while He is near' (Isa. 55:6). This is the time for you to seek the Lord. He is near to you. There is saving grace waiting for you to receive. Just come to Him by faith.

EARS TO HEAR

He who has ears to hear, let him hear
(Luke 14:35).

Those in the crowd following Jesus audibly heard what He said. His message was loud and clear. His words were penetrating and provocative. His demands were strong and shocking. No man ever spoke as He did. No one had ever heard anything like this. But would they actually hear Him? Or would His demands merely go in one ear and out the other?

Tragically, many in the crowd did *not* hear what Jesus said. That was probably true of most. Sure, they heard His actual speech. Their physical ears took in the sound of what

He said. But few heard the true reality and full weight of what He said. They heard Him, but did not hear. They did not listen with spiritual ears. His challenging words were inaudible to them.

To reach their hearts, Jesus issued a final challenge. It is as if He grabbed them by their shoulders and shook them to get their attention. So, Jesus concluded with these words: 'He who has ears to hear, let him hear' (v. 35). What did He mean by this? Did not everyone have ears with which to hear Him? Why would Jesus say this? Of course, they heard Him. Or did they?

Spiritual Ears Needed

This urgent plea by the Lord Jesus called upon the crowd to listen with spiritual ears. He urged them to give their utmost attention to what He had said. Granted, they heard the truth with their natural ears, but they needed to receive what He said with spiritual ears. For these words to proceed from their heads into their hearts, they would need spiritual ears. Only then would His words be internalized into their hearts and souls. Then they had the responsibility to rightly respond. For to hear but not to do, was not to hear at all.

Sadly, most in the crowd that day did not truly hear what He was saying. For different reasons, many in the crowd had turned spiritually deaf ears to His demands. A few heard Him with discerning ears, but only a small percentage of them. Why did so many truly not hear the words of Jesus? Why did they have ears to hear, but did not hear? If this crowd was like most people, a variety of reasons prevented them from hearing what Jesus was truly saying.

Mental Distractions

First, some in the crowd did not hear Jesus because they would have been mentally preoccupied with other matters. They were physically present with Christ, but were mentally absent. Their bodies were there, but their minds were somewhere else. Many in the crowd would have been easily distracted with worldly concerns. Their minds would have been drifting onto various temporal matters. They could have been distracted by matters back at home, with work, family, or even with others present that day.

Jesus said that when the Word goes forth, this would be one of the responses. In the parable of the sower, He explained that many 'hear,' but 'did not hear' (Matt. 13:17). One reason was because when the seed of the word was sown, it fell 'among the thorns' and 'the worry of the world' choked it (Matt. 13:22). Such concerns with the things of this world prevent many from hearing what Jesus said.

Many today are similarly distracted when the gospel is made known. They sit in church under the Word, but their mind is far away. Their thoughts are elsewhere. The Word goes in one ear and out the other. They hear, but do not listen. They daydream under the preaching of the gospel. This truth requires you give strictest attention to what Jesus has said.

Everyone who hears the Word is commanded to be 'quick to hear, slow to speak and slow to anger' (James 1:19). You must strive to be a careful listener when the Word is proclaimed and seek to understand what the Lord is saying. When the Word is spoken, Jesus is speaking—and you must listen. Be slow to argue with His teaching, for excuses will only dull your hearing. Pay keen attention to what you hear from the words of our Lord, for in them is life and salvation.

Physical Limitations

Second, others in the crowd would have been growing physically tired and weak. Most would have gone without food and water for some period of time. That had been the case earlier when Jesus fed the five thousand men plus untold numbers of women and children (John 6:1-14). Food and water were hard to come by in the first century with such a large crowd. Increasing hunger and thirst would have been a barrier to hearing Jesus' teaching. Their feet would have been sore from the walking. Their backs would have ached from standing. Their faces would have been scorched from the glaring hot sun. Their lips would have been parched. These conditions would have made it hard to be attentive to the Word Jesus was preaching that day.

Similarly, many today do not actually hear the Word of God because they are constricted by physical limitations. They have stayed up late on Saturday night, then they come dragging into church on Sunday morning. They are late for the service. They have had little or no breakfast. They have no energy to listen when the Word is being preached. They daydream during the sermon. They tune out of the message. They doze off while the Word is preached. Is it any wonder that they do not receive what they hear?

Emotional Hysterias

Third, still others would have been unable to hear what Jesus said because they were too emotionally involved.

The excitement of the crowd would have whipped them into a euphoric frenzy. The hype would have made them incapable of exercising the rational thought needed to process the message. Their hearts would have outrun their heads. The crowd dynamic would have undoubtedly caused people to be swept up in the adrenaline rush of the moment.

Many in the crowd would have been caught up in the hysteria of looking for the supernatural display of His power. They had heard how He healed the sick. They knew about how He cast out demons. They even heard the reports that He had raised the dead. But this preoccupation with physical miracles would have curbed an appetite for spiritual truth. On one occasion, Jesus withdrew from the people because they wanted to see miracles. He responded, 'Let us go somewhere else to the towns nearby, so that I may preach there also; for that is what I came for' (Mark 1:38). The spiritual priority that Jesus placed upon His earthly ministry was preaching the Word, not performing miracles.

In like manner, there are many people today who do not hear what Jesus teaches in His Word because of their obsession with miracles. They are easily led astray because they want to see a display of the supernatural before their eyes. But this is why they do not hear with their ears. It is their fixation with miracles that makes them completely miss the message.

Such a state of hyper-excitement would have prevented people from hearing the words of Christ. His teaching would have been muted in their ears. As a result, they would have failed to hear what Jesus was saying due to this experience with their emotions.

Could this rush of excitement hold you back from hearing the Word? Maybe you attend a church where frenzied emotions outpace the depth of the intellect. Could it be that the straightforward truth of the Scripture is being crowded out by the revved up emotional highs? If so, you could be easily prevented from hearing the real truth that Jesus is speaking to you. It is crucial to give careful thought to what the Lord is saying in His Word. Do you hear the spiritual truth He proclaims?

Spiritual Indifference

Fourth, others in this crowd would have been spiritually indifferent toward what He was saying. Their overexposure to the truth would have caused them to be apathetic to it. A vaccine gives a small dose of the sickness that prevents someone from contracting the real disease. In like manner, an abundant exposure to the gospel without responding to it would have caused some to be further unresponsive to it. In such a scenario, their heads were full of the truth, but it never penetrated into their hearts. It remained mere head knowledge that had never affected their affections. As a result, the truth never moved their wills to truly believe.

Such people could have easily recited what Jesus preached. They could give an accurate restatement of His words. They knew the nuances of the doctrine that He had taught. They could give a cogent summary of what He had expounded. They could even articulate it to others. But the message Jesus gave never truly penetrated their hearts. The truth had never plunged into their inner soul. It had never revealed their sin. They saw no need for the grace of God in salvation.

These words of life had never brought conviction of sin. The teaching of Christ had never caused them to seek God with all their being. Thus, the invitation of Christ had never been answered by a surrendered will.

Maybe that is where you are. Perhaps you are well taught in the teaching of Christ and even have a head full of sound doctrine. You can give an adequate explanation of the Christian faith. You have a Bible on your desk, but not in your inner being. Maybe you are even involved in teaching the truth to others. But could it be that this truth has not gone deeper in your life? Has it ever progressed beyond your mind and into your heart? If this describes you, ask God to bring the truth home to your heart. Ask Him to give you ears to hear. Ask Him to take it from your head to permeate your very heart and soul.

Personal Deception

Fifth, still others in the multitude would have heard what Jesus said, but wrongly assumed the message was for others, and not for them. Many deceived themselves into presuming that they were right with God. But in reality, this was far from the case. Because they were a part of this religious crowd, they believed they must be in the kingdom of God. They had this close proximity to Jesus. They even walked next to Him. By hearing the words of Christ, they came to assume that they also believed the message.

But nothing could have been further from the truth. They were within steps of Jesus, but did not know Him.

They walked alongside Jesus, but did not follow Him. They beheld Him, but did not believe in Him. They heard Him, but did not heed Him.

Untold numbers today are just as self-deceived as these first-century listeners. Countless church members perceive that because they attend church, they must be acceptable to God. Tragically, they have an empty hope of a salvation that they do not personally possess. The reason they assume they are a child of God is due to their association with other believers. The sad reality is, such individuals have never come all the way to Christ. They have assumed a relationship with Christ based upon their own terms. But they have never denied themselves, taken up a cross, and followed Christ.

Where Are You?

Where are you with the Lord? Are you alive in Christ? Have you believed in Him for your salvation? Have you been given spiritual ears to hear this great message? To truly hear and understand the gospel, you must have this spiritual hearing from above. It must go from your head to your heart, resulting in true belief and commitment to Christ. You must see your need for Him and admit your only hope is found in Him.

Seek Him today while He may be found. Ask Him to open your deaf ears and give you the faith to believe these words. Is there something holding you back from coming all the way to Him? Have you admitted your need and reliance on Him alone, forsaking everything else? Will you take this decisive step of faith and come to Christ? He stands ready to save you even today.

LASTING WORDS

He who has ears to hear, let him hear
(Luke 14:35).

Whenever someone of great wisdom speaks, his words should
have a lasting effect. Given the prominence of this individual,
his message should be taken carefully to heart. This being
so, how much more must the words of Jesus Christ weigh
heavily upon us. Jesus is the greatest individual ever to walk
the earth. He was God in human flesh—the Son of God,
the Son of Man. As the long promised Messiah, the supreme
importance of His teaching cannot be overstated. Whatever
He spoke must command our lives and direct our steps.

As the One sent from heaven, Jesus spoke the very words the Father gave Him to speak. Jesus claimed, 'For I did not speak on my own initiative, but the Father Himself who sent me has given me a commandment as to what to say and what to speak' (John 12:49). This says, whoever receives the words of Jesus receives the very words of God. But rejecting Jesus' words—failing to act upon them—is a soul-endangering matter. To refuse the words of Jesus is to refuse the only way of salvation.

Given this reality, this crowd must truly 'hear' what Jesus says. The truth that He spoke must resonate deep within them. It was one thing for them to hear with physical ears what Jesus said. But it would be something else for them to hear with spiritual ears. They needed to listen to His words with receptive hearts. Life and death hang in the balance—as do heaven and hell.

This same message from Jesus must reverberate in your soul this moment. It must seize your mind and grab hold of your heart. You must receive His message with your whole being—with your mind, emotions, and will.

Whatever Jesus says requires a response from you. Let us consider what this response necessitates.

What You Must *Know*

First, if you are to follow Jesus Christ, you must *know* the truth. Specifically, you must know about *the eternal deity of Jesus Christ*. You must know who the Lord Jesus Christ is—the eternal Son of the living God. He was sent by God the Father into this world on a divine mission to rescue lost sinners from eternal destruction. He was born of a virgin and entered the human race as the God-Man—truly God and truly man.

You must know about *the sinless life of Jesus*. He was born under the Law of God (Gal. 4:4) in order to obey its commands. This is the very same Law that we have repeatedly broken. By His perfect obedience to the Law, He fulfilled all righteousness (Matt. 3:15). In so doing, He achieved the righteousness that we need to find acceptance with God. It is this righteousness that is credited to all unrighteous sinners who believe in Him.

You must know about *the sin-bearing death of Jesus*. Being sinless, He was qualified to die in the place of guilty sinners. He was lifted up on a Roman cross in order to become the sacrifice for sin. In His death, Jesus bore our sins in His body (1 Pet. 2:24) and secured the salvation of sinners. He is the only way of salvation. Jesus said: 'I am the way, and the truth, and the life; no one comes to the Father but through Me' (John 14:6). Faith in Jesus alone leads to heaven. The Bible says: 'There is salvation in no one else; for there is no other name under heaven that has been given among men by which we must be saved' (Acts 4:12).

You must know about *the bodily resurrection of Jesus*. After His death, He was buried in a borrowed tomb (John 19:38). But on the third day, He was raised from the dead (1 Cor. 15:4). This resurrection was definitive proof from God that Christ's death was the perfect sacrifice to take away the sins of all who believe in Him (Rom. 4:25). He then ascended back to the right hand of God the Father (Acts 1:9-11). He is now enthroned on high, possessing all authority in heaven and earth. The Bible declares: 'WHOEVER SHALL CALL UPON THE NAME OF THE LORD WILL BE SAVED' (Rom.10:13).

You must also know about *the gospel invitation of Jesus*. Jesus called to the crowd two thousand years ago to 'repent and believe in the gospel' (Mark 1:15). He later pleaded, 'Come to Me, all who are weary and heavy-laden, and I will give you rest. Take My yoke upon you and learn from Me, for I am gentle and humble in heart, and YOU WILL FIND REST FOR YOUR SOULS. For My yoke is easy and My burden is light' (Matt. 11:28-30). Here, He demands that you die to yourself. You must know that you must come to Him with complete trust. He commands the crowd to come to Him by faith alone.

What You Must *Feel*

Second, if you are to become a follower of Christ, you must *feel* your desperate need of Him. Your conscience must cause you to perceive the haunting guilt of your sin. Your heart must be alarmed with the sobering realization that you are perishing without Jesus. You must be 'pierced to the heart' (Acts 2:37) by the Holy Spirit, because of what you know about your spiritual bankruptcy. You must feel this sharp pain before you can be a genuine disciple of Christ.

You must feel *the conviction of the Holy Spirit*. The Spirit has come into the world to convict you of your need for Christ. Jesus said, the Spirit 'will convict the world concerning sin and righteousness and judgment; concerning sin, because they do not believe in Me; and concerning righteousness, because I go to the Father and you no longer see Me; and concerning judgment, because the ruler of this world has been judged' (John 16:8-11). The Spirit must convince you of the guilt of your sin. Mind you, this will not be a pleasant experience. No one flippantly skips through the narrow gate that leads into the kingdom. No one giggles into God's presence. Jesus said, 'Blessed are those who mourn' (Matt. 5:4). Such brokenness of spirit is the only proper response to your spiritual poverty before God (James 4:9).

Do you feel the hopelessness of your condition without faith in Christ? Do you sense your uncleanness before the Lord? Do you see that you fall short when measured next to God's perfect holiness?

In addition, the Spirit must make you feel *the amazing love of God's grace.* He offers salvation to you this moment. Despite your unworthiness, He freely extends grace to you. The Spirit causes your heart to melt as you learn to what great lengths God has gone to deliver sinners from eternal destruction. Are you moved by His all-forgiving love that desires to receive you? Regardless of how unworthy you are, Christ still calls you to come to Him.

What You Must *Do*

Third, if you are to follow Christ, you must *do* something. It is not enough that you know these truths of the gospel. Nor is it enough that you feel your need for Jesus Christ. You must take the final step—the decisive step of faith. You must act upon what you know and are persuaded to be true.

As an act of your will, you must *repent of your sins and entrust your life to Jesus (Mark 1:15).* He alone can save you from your sins. You must turn away from living for yourself. You must renounce your love affair with this world. You must denounce your indifference toward God. You must turn away from this path of destruction. You must turn to Jesus Christ and entrust yourself to Him.

You must take *the active step of faith* to commit your life to Jesus Christ. Faith trusts Him alone for the forgiveness of sin and the obtaining of His righteousness. Turn to Him for the forgiveness of your sins. Trust Him for His perfect righteousness. Look to Jesus with the eyes of faith. Rest in His perfect sacrifice for sins at the cross.

The Lord Jesus Christ waits for you to come to Him. He will receive you into His arms of grace. He is the 'friend of sinners' (Matt. 11:19). He is a physician who has come not for those who are well, but for those who are sick (Luke 5:31). Confess to Him how sick you are in your sin. He will make you whole.

Will you submit your life to Him? Will you deny yourself? Will you take up your cross? Will you follow Him? Jesus would warmly welcome you. He says, 'the one who comes to Me I will certainly not cast out' (John 6:37).

Take That Step of Faith

The gates of paradise are swung wide open. You are invited to enter through the narrow gate. The Lord Jesus will receive you to Himself. He is calling you this very moment. Take that step of faith and come to Him.

If you will believe in Jesus, He will lift from you the heavy weight of your sin. He will place His yoke upon you, which is 'easy' and 'light' (Matt. 11:30). Why continue under the burden of your sin? Jesus will remove your sin and replace it with His matchless presence in your life.

There is a sense of urgency about making this commitment to Christ. You must do so now. Your life is passing. The world is perishing. Time is short. The hour is late. Death is coming. The judgment is looming. Heaven is prepared. Hell is real. Eternity is beckoning.

He who has ears to hear, let him hear.

I Am a Disciple

I came across a striking poem several years ago. It is entitled 'I Am a Disciple'. Pay attention to the life-giving truths communicated therein. May this be your confession. May this be your testimony.

> The die has been cast.
> I have stepped over the line.
> The decision has been made.
> I am a disciple of Jesus Christ.
>
> I will not look up,
>   let up,
>   slow down,
>   back away,
>   or be still.
> I no longer need preeminence,
>   prosperity,
>   position,
>   promotions,
>   plaudits,
>   or popularity.
> I do not have to be right,
>   first,
>   tops,

recognized,
praised,
regarded,
or rewarded.
I now live by faith,
love by patience,
live by prayer,
and labor by power.
My pace is set.
My gait is fast.
My goal is Heaven.
My road is narrow.
My way is rough.
My companions few.
My Guide reliable.
My mission clear.

I cannot be bought,
compromised,
deterred,
lured away,
turned back,
diluted,
or delayed.
I will not flinch in the face of sacrifice.
I will not hesitate in the presence of adversity.
I will not negotiate at the table of the enemy.
I will not ponder at the pool of popularity,
nor meander in the maze of mediocrity.
I will not give up,
back up,
let up,

or shut up until I have prayed up,
preached up,
stored up
and stayed up the cause of Christ.
I am a disciple of Jesus Christ.

I must go until He returns,
   give until I drop,
   preach until all know,
   and work until He comes.
And when He comes to get His own,
   He will have no trouble recognizing me.
My colors are flying high,
   and they are clear for all to see.
I am a disciple of Jesus Christ.

Are you a disciple of Jesus Christ? Step out of the crowd. Come to Him and receive His salvation. It is a free gift. I must tell you, it will cost you everything. However, you will gain everything—everything you need—both now and forever.

Christian Focus Publications

Our mission statement—STAYING FAITHFUL

In dependence upon God we seek to impact the world through literature faithful to His infallible Word, the Bible. Our aim is to ensure that the Lord Jesus Christ is presented as the only hope to obtain forgiveness of sin, live a useful life and look forward to heaven with Him.

Our Books are published in four imprints:

CHRISTIAN
FOCUS

popular works including biographies, commentaries, basic doctrine and Christian living.

CHRISTIAN
HERITAGE

books representing some of the best material from the rich heritage of the church.

MENTOR

books written at a level suitable for Bible College and seminary students, pastors, and other serious readers. The imprint includes commentaries, doctrinal studies, examination of current issues and church history.

CF4•K

children's books for quality Bible teaching and for all age groups: Sunday school curriculum, puzzle and activity books; personal and family devotional titles, biographies and inspirational stories—Because you are never too young to know Jesus!

Christian Focus Publications Ltd,
Geanies House, Fearn, Ross-shire,
IV20 1TW, Scotland, United Kingdom.
www.christianfocus.com